NEWER IDEALS OF PEACE

JANE ADDAMS

Newer Ideals of Peace

INTRODUCTION BY
BERENICE A. CARROLL
AND
CLINTON F. FINK

University of Illinois Press
URBANA AND CHICAGO

First Illinois edition, 2007
Introduction © Berenice A. Carroll and Clinton F. Fink
All rights reserved

∞ This book is printed on acid-free paper.

Library of Congress Cataloging-in-Publication Data
Addams, Jane, 1860–1935.
Newer ideals of peace / Jane Addams; with an introduction by
Berenice A. Carroll and Clinton F. Fink.
p.   cm.
Includes bibliographical references and index.
ISBN-13: 978-0-252-03105-2 (ISBN 13 / cloth : alk. paper)
ISBN-10: 0-252–03105–9 (ISBN 10 / cloth : alk. paper)
ISBN-13: 978–0–252–07345–8 (ISBN 13 / paper : alk. paper)
ISBN-10: 0-252-07345-2 (ISBN 10 / paper : alk. paper)
1. Political participation—United States.
2. Municipal government—United States.
3. Working class—United States.
4. Peace. 5. Social justice.
I. Carroll, Berenice A. II. Fink, Clinton F. III. Title.
HN64.A25   2007
306.2'0973—dc22   2005013923

to

Hull-House

and

its Neighbors

Contents

Introduction
to the Illinois Edition

BERENICE A. CARROLL
AND CLINTON F. FINK

[The founders] depended upon penalties, coercion, compulsion, remnants of military codes, to hold the community together. . . . Having looked to the sword for independence from oppressive governmental control, they came to regard the sword as an essential part of the government they had succeeded in establishing. (*Newer Ideals of Peace,* pp. 21–22)

. . . to distinguish between a social order founded upon law enforced by authority and that other social order which includes liberty of individual action and complexity of group development. The latter social order would not suppress the least germ of promise, of growth and variety, but would nurture all into a full and varied life. (p. 118)

. . . spontaneous and fraternal action as virile and widespread as war itself is the only method by which substitutes for the war virtues may be discovered. (p. 118)

This reissue of *Newer Ideals of Peace* (*NIP*), in the University of Illinois Press collection of works by Jane Addams, appears just short of the centennial anniversary of its first printing in December 1906.[1] When it appeared it was widely reviewed and warmly welcomed in surprisingly diverse quarters. Despite some dismissive remarks—by Theodore Roosevelt among others—most commentaries ranged from serious but friendly critique to laudatory and even fulsome praise.

Unless otherwise indicated, all page number citations to *Newer Ideals of Peace* in the text of this introduction refer to the page numbers in this University of Illinois Press edition. For corresponding pagination in the 1906 edition, see pages lxxiv–lxxvii.

William James, the eminent psychologist and philosopher, wrote in a letter to Addams on February 12, 1907, "I find it hard to express the good it has done me in opening new points of view and annihilating old ones. New perspectives of hope! I don't care about this detail or that—it is the *new setting of questions.* Yours is a deeply original mind, and all so quiet and harmless! Yet revolutionary in the extreme, and I should suspect that this very work would act as a ferment through long years to come" (emphasis in the original).[2]

Though little remembered in the period between World War II and the present, *Newer Ideals of Peace* may justly be regarded as the most important and innovative work of peace theory in the first decades of the twentieth century and a primary source of ideas more widely espoused in later years. In it Addams sought to break out of the traditional *anti-war* focus of conventional pacifism in her time, rejecting what she called "negative peace" and declaring: "one despairs of arousing enthusiasm for peace unless it is done more positively than any of the present peace societies are able to do it."[3]

In the effort to present ideas and analyses that would enable peace movements to pursue a more positive conception of peace, Addams addressed a wide range of issues, from the undemocratic leanings of those she called "the founders" to the militarization of society and governance, the conceptualization of "negative peace" and "positive peace," the search for "moral substitutes for war," the relationships of labor and capitalism to peace and war, the public responsibilities and rights of women, and the roots of peace in the cosmopolitan neighborhoods of the poor, or what we might call "internationalization from below." In this introduction, we address the original, complex, and often controversial character of Addams's ideas in *Newer Ideals of Peace,* the paradoxes of praise and neglect to which it has been subject, and the legacy it offers for the present.

I. Genesis

Addams had first used the title "The Newer Ideals of Peace" in two lectures published in the *Chautauqua Assembly Herald* in July 1902 (see n. 3). Her book entitled *Newer Ideals of Peace* (*NIP*) was published four and a half years later as a volume in Macmillan's series, the *Citizens*

Library of Economics, Politics, and Sociology, edited by Richard T. Ely. In October 1902, after her first book (*Democracy and Social Ethics*) had appeared in the same series and sold well, Macmillan invited her to provide them with another. At Ely's insistence, she suggested the idea for a second book in his series, using the title of her Chautauqua lectures. Given an enthusiastic reception by the publishers, Addams signed a contract for the book in January 1903, worked on it over the next three years, gave a series of lectures on it in the summer of 1906, and finally submitted it for publication in September 1906. The official publication date was set for January 16, 1907, but Addams was eager to have copies of the book in hand to use in lobbying for more lenient immigration legislation. Accordingly *Newer Ideals of Peace* first appeared in December 1906 in a small number of proof and review copies with a 1906 copyright and publication date. In a letter of December 12, 1906, she reported to Macmillan that she had given a proof copy to President Theodore Roosevelt and requested a few more to give to key legislators in Washington.

Later printings, with a 1907 copyright, appeared in 1907, 1911, and 1915.[4] The book fell out of print for decades after 1931 and was omitted from the extensive Garland Press reprint collection, *The Garland Library of War and Peace,* in which other works on peace by Addams did appear.[5] Instead, *Newer Ideals of Peace* appeared in 1972 in a facsimile reprint series, *The Peace Movement in America* (New York: Jerome Ozer). Recent years, however, have seen a notable revival of interest in it. An electronic version was entered on-line during 1996–99. In 2003 the book was reprinted in the four-volume hardcover set issued by Thoemmes Press (see n. 95). In July 2004 a trade paperback edition was published by the Anza Classics Library as *Newer Ideals of Peace: The Moral Substitutes for War.*[6]

The ideas about peace and pacifism, democracy, and militarism that Addams presented in *Newer Ideals of Peace* were developed over the ten-year period prior to its publication. They were grounded in ideas about social justice, humanitarianism, and the cooperative potential of the urban immigrant poor—ideas that she had been maturing for at least two decades, especially in connection with her work at Hull-House beginning in 1889. Addams noted that two chapters of the book and parts of two others were first published in separate articles (p. 3).

Other previously published materials found their way, usually in elaborated form, into the final version of the book.[7]

Addams's nephew and biographer James Linn cited a brief entry in one of her notebooks written as early as 1896 in which she wondered whether the "forced 'internationalism' developed [among diverse immigrants] in American cities . . . [might] be made an effective instrument in the cause of world-peace."[8] This became a major theme in *Newer Ideals of Peace.*

In support of the anti-imperialist campaign triggered by the U.S. acquisition of the Philippines in 1899, Addams gave a talk in April of that year on "Democracy or Militarism."[9] There she introduced her concern with the issues of militarism and indicated her broad conception of peace, associating it with democratic, internationalist humanitarianism. "We must also remember that peace has come to mean a larger thing. It is no longer merely absence of war but the unfolding of life processes which are making for a common development."[10]

The two Chautauqua lectures on "The Newer Ideals of Peace" in July 1902 (see n. 3) contained many ideas that were later discussed in *Newer Ideals of Peace.* In the first lecture, Addams presented a critique of the peace movement's appeals to sympathy and prudence, which she later expanded in Chapter I of the book. She also discussed the appeal to the sense of human solidarity, asserting that "when we once surround human life with the same kind of heroism and admiration that we have surrounded war, we can say that this sense is having such an outlet that war will become impossible."[11]

In her second 1902 Chautauqua lecture Addams spoke of a new internationalist conception of patriotism: "Let us imagine that [great numbers of young men in this country] shall have the kind of patriotism which the intermingling of the nations has forced upon us, instead of the patriotism which prevailed when each nation had to regard the others as enemies."[12]

Addams then went on to speak of new "positive ideals" of peace. She urged her audience to imagine that "the newer ideals of peace should come to be something so positive" that young men would no longer seek war as the path to heroism, but would rather conceive of "some such positive ideal" of heroism as the effort to "make possible a higher type of life."[13] She also made clear in this lecture that a positive ideal of peace must encompass a concern for the conditions of labor for both children and working adults. She dwelt at length on the issue of sweatshops, and though her focus was on the prevalence of sweated labor in the United States at that time, her words resonate as strikingly familiar in the global anti-sweatshop movement today: "We may get to the point where we are more cautious of the garments we wear, as to the method of their making."[14]

In the spring of 1903 Addams lectured on "A Moral Substitute for War" at the Ethical Culture Society in Chicago.[15] She continued elaborating this idea in addresses at the International Peace Congress held in Boston in 1904.[16] Then, in her prefatory note in 1906, she identified this as a central theme of *Newer Ideals of Peace:* "These studies in *the gradual development of the moral substitutes for war* have been made in the industrial quarter of a cosmopolitan city where the morality exhibits marked social and international aspects" (p. 3, emphasis added).

Undergirding Addams's elaboration of this theme in *Newer Ideals* was a complex, often surprising, critique of what she named "negative peace" and of the militarized character of American society in the twentieth century.

II. The Critique of "Negative Peace" and of the "Founders"

In the post–World War II field of peace studies, Norwegian sociologist and leading peace researcher Johan Galtung initiated discussion of the concepts of "negative peace" and "positive peace" in several papers published in the 1960s. These concepts, which have become central to contemporary peace theory, are often attributed to him.

But Jane Addams had used the term "negative peace" nearly sixty years earlier in *Newer Ideals of Peace,* and though she did not use the phrase "positive peace" as such, the "positive ideals of peace" that she spoke of in 1902 were elaborated in *Newer Ideals* and correspond closely with present-day interpretations of that concept. The history of the terms in the subsequent decades has not been traced, though both Quincy Wright and Martin Luther King, Jr. had already used them, before Galtung did.[17] Over the course of that history, the term "positive peace" has had quite varied meanings, but in general, the term "negative peace" has been defined mainly as the absence of war, conflict, or violence.

Addams expressed this idea in 1899, as noted above, in saying that the concept of peace had become "no longer merely absence of war." But in *Newer Ideals of Peace*, Addams used the term "negative peace" also in a different and more complex sense, to characterize certain older ideals of peace that she held to be negative or inadequate. In this sense her use of the term brought with it the implication that peace should be understood to encompass more adequate and positive goals and principles.

A remarkable feature of Addams's argument was her sharp critique of the intellectual, political, and military heritage of the eighteenth-century philosophers and founders of modern political and social institutions, as well as the traditional advocates of peace. She contrasted "the claims of the newer, more aggressive ideals of peace" with an "older dovelike ideal" (p. 5). Philosophers of the past (among whom she singled out Immanuel Kant, Jeremy Bentham, and Thomas Buckle) were, she wrote, "the first to sigh for *negative peace* which they declared would be 'eternal'" (p. 15, emphasis added). Skeptical of "universal peace" and "permanent peace," or "the old dogmatic peace," Addams found such ideas "discouraging" in what she held to be their abstract and static character (pp. 6–7).

While she expressed admiration for Leo Tolstoy, Vassili Verestchagin, and Jean de Bloch, who exposed the horrors and costs of war, as well as for "the untiring efforts of the advocates of peace through many years" (p. 6), she suspected that these approaches embodied a fatal error: "Here it is quite possible that the mistake is being repeated which the old annalists of history made when they never failed to chronicle the wars and calamities which harassed their contemporaries, although, while the few indulged in fighting, the mass of them peacefully prosecuted their daily toil and followed their own conceptions of kindliness and equity" (pp. 6–7).

For Addams, the focus on war itself, on the warriors and the values associated with war and conquest—"the flimsy stuff called national honor, glory, and prestige" (p. 64)—perpetuated the dominance of "the older military virtues" and habits in society and obscured the processes of dynamic evolution towards a more positive kind of peace.

Addams's critique, however, extended beyond attention to war, to address many of the central tenets of government and democracy: "To follow this newer humanitarianism even through its obvious manifestations requires at the very outset a definite abandonment of the eighteenth-century philosophy upon which so much of our present democratic theory and philanthropic activity depends" (p. 18). She challenged the "historic and doctrinaire method" of the founders for its inadequacy "when it attempts to deal with growing and human institutions," especially as manifested in the failures of municipal administration in her time (p. 20).

The founders, she argued, "with all their fine talk of the 'natural man' and what he would accomplish when he obtained freedom and equality, did not really trust the people after all" (p. 21). She reproached them for "timidly" adopting the principles of English law, more concerned "with the guarding of prerogative and with the rights of property than with the spontaneous life of the people" (p. 21).[18] They distanced themselves from the daily life of the people, she contended, and by modeling their governmental machinery on European traditions, "failed to provide the vehicle for a vital and genuinely organized expression of the popular will" through effective local self-government (p. 22).

Addams questioned the founders' abstract notion of "the natural man," as "a creature of their sympathetic imaginations," and she argued in a passage that would be well to heed today: "Because their idealism was of the type that is afraid of experience, these founders refused to look at the difficulties and blunders which a self-governing people were sure to encounter, and insisted that, if only the people had freedom, they would walk continuously in the paths of justice and righteousness" (p. 20).

Thus Addams makes clear that, rather than holding a naïve faith in "the people," she was well aware that they would face difficulties, might make blunders, and might not always act with "justice and righteousness." She faulted the founders for their reliance on institutional models that failed to give scope to *local* self-governance, and their unrealistic confidence in an ideal of "freedom" *alone,* understood as the protection of individual "natural rights," and in particular property rights, through the traditions of English law.

This reflected the influence in her thought of the socialist critique of individualism, touching also on the exploitation of an "unemployed and unskilled" international labor force. She attributed the vast and unprecedented migrations of people around the globe to the confluence of an eighteenth-century "creed of individual liberty" and the expansion of free market capitalism: "The modern system of industry and commerce presupposes freedom of occupation, of travel, and residence; even more, it unhappily rests in a large measure upon the assumption of a body of the unemployed and the unskilled, ready to be absorbed or dropped according to the demands of production" (p. 25). Situating these developments in the context of eighteenth-century "natural rights" doctrine (p. 25), she called upon Josiah Royce's critique of notions of "inborn rights." Addams argued that human rights are not "inalienable." She did not, of course, mean to undercut the struggle for human rights, but rather to emphasize that they were "hard-won in the tragic processes of experience" (p. 21).[19] In a remark deeply resonant today, she warned that "these painfully acquired rights must be carefully cherished or they may at any moment slip out of our hands" (p. 21).

Addams was much less confident than many pacifists and liberals that democracy, as constituted in her time, would necessarily diminish war: "Immoderate and uncontrolled desires are at the root of most national as well as of most individual crimes, and a large number of persons may be moved by unworthy ambitions quite as easily as a few" (p. 123). In 1902, she had considered "commercial interdependence" of nations as a force for internationalization and peace, but in *Newer Ideals of Peace* she expressed concern that a democratic electorate holding "the commercial view of life" would give moral sanction to expansionist policies (p. 123).

Addams argued that "the worship of success, so long dominant in America, has taught the majority of our citizens to count only accomplishment and to make little inquiry concerning methods" (p. 71). Moral consciousness is paralyzed, she suggested, "when the belief is once established that success is its own justification" (p. 78). In words again highly relevant today, she wrote: "The nation which is accustomed to condone the questionable business methods of a rich man because of his success, will find no difficulty in obscuring the moral issues involved in any undertaking that is successful. It becomes easy to deny the moral basis of self-government and to substitute militarism" (p. 123).

In using the term "militarism," Addams's analysis was directed not only at the growth and increasing influence of military institutions as such, but even more at the pervasive adoption of military values and models in all aspects of "civilian" society. Thus negative peace, for Addams, implied not only the absence of war, but the failure to overcome a perverted heritage of attitudes and institutions derived from wars and conquest in the past.

III. "Militarism" and Its Opponents

"Militarism," as a focus of attack by pacifists and socialists, is a familiar concept today, though its usage varies widely. The term dates back at least to the early nineteenth century, when its first use has been attributed to Victorine de Chastenay, who, writing of the situation in France under Napoleon in 1812, commented on "the ravages of conscription and those which resulted from the tendency towards the success of militarism."[20] Volker R. Berghahn suggests that the idea was well established before the twentieth century to denote a condition "wherever and whenever military considerations exerted a decisive influence on civilian government."[21] Berghahn credited Herbert Spencer with "what appears to have been the first systematic analysis of militarism," but Spencer called it rather the "militant type of society." Spencer enlarged his conception to refer not only to military influence on government, but also to the mobilization of "indirect aid of all who cannot fight" for support of the military by the rest of society, requiring a system of centralization and regimentation affecting the whole community.[22]

Addams was likely familiar with Spencer's sociology, though she did not refer to him in her writings and, as shown by Sondra Herman, differed from him significantly in her theoretical analysis.[23] In her early treatment of the subject of militarism, Addams was clearly more influenced by the ideas of the socialist and anti-imperialist movements than by Spencer. In her 1899 speech on "Democracy or Militarism," Addams argued that the working classes had been the foremost opponents of militarism and the leading advocates of a "new conception of peace": "it is perhaps natural that the first men to formulate it and give it international meaning should have been workingmen, who have always realized, however feebly and vaguely they may have expressed it, that it is they who in all ages have borne the heaviest burden of privation and suffering imposed on the world by the military spirit."[24]

She cited the commitment of the International Association of Workingmen in London in 1864 to a common interest uniting them above race prejudice and national divisions; the declaration of its third congress, in Brussels in 1868, that "the workers resist all war as systematic murder"; and the statement by President Samuel Gompers of the American Federation of Labor that "with the success of imperialism the decadence of our republic will have already set in." "Organization," she declared, is the only hope of the workingman, "but it must be kept distinct from militarism, which can never be made a democratic instrument."[25]

Without seeking to define militarism here, Addams appears to identify it with "all pride of conquest," "the military spirit," imperialism, war, and standing armies. These were indeed the aspects of militarism that, along with expanding military expenditures and influence in government and the economy, were addressed in the first decades of the twentieth century by both pacifists and socialists.

Thus Rosa Luxemburg, addressing the International Socialist Congress in Paris in 1900, pointed out that declarations of the international congresses of Paris in 1889, Brussels in 1891, and London 1896 had already condemned militarism as one of the most dangerous features of the capitalist order and demanded the abolition of standing armies, the establishment of international courts of justice, and the right of the peoples to decide about war and peace. Luxemburg urged adoption of a new resolution presented by the commissions on militarism and colonialism. They had met jointly in the conviction that "militarism and colonialism today are only two different sides of the same world political phenomenon" to stimulate redoubled efforts through youth organization, education, and uncompromising socialist opposition in all parliaments to budgetary outlays for militarism and colonial expeditions on land and sea.[26]

These ideas were developed and expanded by Luxemburg and her comrade Karl Liebknecht in the course of the following years. Luxemburg later put forward a strikingly prescient analysis of the role of militarism as "a province of capitalist accumulation." She and Liebknecht also made references to the growing influence of militarism in society. But although Luxemburg in 1900 had spoken of militarism as "the deadly enemy of all culture" and called for "collective daily struggle against it,"[27] and Liebknecht declared that "[M]ilitarism makes its appearance as a system which *saturates the whole public and private life of our people with the militarist spirit,*"[28] the specific issues they addressed centered on military and colonial institutions and policies, rather than the broader and deeper manifestations of militarism in modern culture.[29]

In the years after 1899, Addams went beyond Luxemburg and Liebknecht, expanding her analysis to address the pervasive militarization of civilian society itself. It was not merely forcible control or military influence in government and policy, nor military and colonial expeditions abroad, nor explicitly militarist organizations and institutions, but the domination and distortion of all aspects of human life by military values, habits, practices, institutional models, interests, and ideologies that she began to discern as a major problem in society.

In *Newer Ideals of Peace,* Addams presented this idea for the first time in its full scope. Most important are her chapters on "Survivals of Militarism in City Government" and "Militarism and Industrial Legislation," but there are also sections throughout the book on the significance and influence of military values and war habits on capitalism, the labor movement, industrial relations, children, and male-female relations. Her chapters on immigrants and women in city government, protection of children, and group morality in the labor movement, as well as her concluding chapter, "Passing of the War Virtues," contrast the negative consequences of militarist tendencies with the prospects of what she called "the newer, aggressive ideals of peace." Her analysis of militarization and her alternative conceptions of what we now call "positive peace" are tightly interwoven, complex, and multidimensional.

IV. The Critique of Militarized Society

Addams's analysis of the militarization of civilian society began with her critique of the ideas of the founders, touched upon above. The ideas of negative peace which she attributed to them were grounded, she thought, in their fascination with war and military virtues: "They depended upon penalties, coercion, compulsion, remnants of military codes, to hold the community together; and it may be possible to trace much of the maladministration of our cities to these survivals. . . . In the hour of danger we revert to the military and legal type although they become less and less appropriate to city life in proportion as the city grows more complex, more varied in resources and more highly organized, and is, therefore in greater need of a more diffused local autonomy" (pp. 21–22).

Addams repeatedly emphasized this need for local autonomy and self-government, and reproached the founders for lacking "a well-grounded belief in social capacity and the efficiency of the popular will" (p. 21). Addams saw this distrust of the people as both misguided and infused with traditional reliance on military techniques and values, "the old restraints which government has traditionally enlisted in its behalf," reinforced by the experiences of the Revolutionary War: "Having looked to the sword for independence from oppressive governmental control, they came to regard the sword as an essential part of the government they had succeeded in establishing" (p. 22).

These militarized attitudes, Addams argued, were counterproductive for the development of democratic institutions both in government and in class relations. She discerned "survivals of the virtues of a warlike period" in municipal politics and the labor movement and other "dangers of class morality" (p. 18) including attitudes of class and ethnic superiority. Clinging to the traditions of the militarist past had led to a false sense of superiority of the Anglo-Saxon over the "political ideals of the Celtic, Germanic, Latin, and Slavic immigrants who have successively come to us; and in our overwhelming ambition to remain Anglo-Saxon, we have fallen into the Anglo-Saxon temptation of governing all peoples by one standard" (p. 28). The imperial practices that allowed an Englishman to "control the destinies of the Egyptian child toiling in the cotton factory in Alexandria, and of the half-starved Parsee working in the opium fields of North India," were grounded in the view that these peoples were "inferior" (p. 29). Such attitudes of superiority and inferiority were scorned by Addams not only in the colonial or racial contexts but in regard to the treatment of children, contempt for labor, and even a fundamental "contempt for human nature" that she regarded as a part of the heritage of military conquest (p. 118).

The survivals of militarism, Addams argued, also distort our ideas of courage and patriotism. The conception of patriotism, "although as genuine as ever before, is too much dressed in the trappings of the past and continually carries us back to its beginnings in military prowess and defence" (p. 119). Traditional patriotism, Addams maintained, "is totally inadequate to help us through the problems which current life develops" (p. 120).

To embody "the real interest of the nation," she wrote, "the conception of patriotism [must be] progressive." To be worthy of "a great cosmopolitan nation," such a progressive patriotism would have to go beyond both "the patriotism of descent" (the clan) and the patriotism of "possession of a like territory" (p. 120). Patriotism would become, in short, internationalist. Uncertain how to express this "new internationalism," she thought it might be necessary to adopt the "rather absurd" term "cosmic patriotism" to express the force of a sentiment "strong enough to move masses of men out of their narrow national considerations and cautions into new reaches of human effort and affection" (pp. 130–31).

In marked contrast to Rosa Luxemburg's analysis of militarism as "a province of capitalist accumulation," Addams sometimes spoke of capitalist industrialism as fundamentally opposed to militarism. In the municipal context: "When the State protects its civic resources, as it formerly defended its citizens in time of war, industrialism versus militarism comes to be nurture versus conquest" (p. 18). In the colonial context: "Militarism undertakes to set in order, to suppress and to govern, if necessary to destroy, while industrialism undertakes to liberate latent forces, to reconcile them to new conditions, to demonstrate that their aroused activities can no longer follow caprice, but must fit into a larger order of life" (p. 122).

But Addams was not an uncritical admirer of industrialism and did not see it as inherently opposed to militarism. For one thing, she was well aware of the commercial interests of "the industries now tributary to the standing armies and organization of warfare" (p. 126) and of the role of such interests in promoting militarism and war. "Unrestricted commercialism," she wrote, "is an excellent preparation for governmental aggression" (p. 123).

She associated the more positive image of industrialism with the idea of constructive labor and the labor movement: "Workingmen dream of an industrialism which shall be the handmaid of a commerce ministering to an increased power of consumption among the producers of the world, binding them together in a genuine internationalism" (p. 64).

But she saw the emergence of a very different contemporary reality. The prototype of modern commerce and industrialism, she asserted, was "slavery and vassalage." It was "founded upon a contempt for the worker" and recognized only such animal wants as "food and shelter and the cost of replacement" to justify low wages (p. 64). Moreover, though the soldier now obeys the merchant whom he formerly looked down upon, "he still looks down upon the laborer as a man who is engaged in a business inferior to his own, as someone who is dull and passive and ineffective" (p. 123). Thus the actual development of commerce and industry had turned out to be largely contrary to the interests of the workers and not at all in accord with their internationalist aims: "Existing commerce has long ago reached its international stage, but it has been the result of business aggression and constantly appeals for military defense and for the forcing of new markets. . . . It has logically lent itself to warfare, and is, indeed, the modern representative of conquest" (p. 64). In place of such theories of industrial, commercial, and "democratic" peace, Addams turned to ideas of "moral substitutes for war," positive peace, and a worldwide movement towards peace and internationalization from below.

V. Seeking "Moral Substitutes for War"

"These studies in the gradual development of the moral substitutes for war," Addams wrote in her prefatory note for *Newer Ideals of Peace*, "are held together by a conviction that has been maturing through many years" (p. 3). Though Addams noted in the introduction that William James had "lately reminded us" of the need to "discover in the social realm the moral equivalent for war," her words were carefully chosen. While James has frequently been credited with originating this concept, and Addams's remark is often interpreted as acknowledging indebtedness to him for the idea, she was careful to say only that James had "lately *reminded* us" of this need.

James's famed essay, "The Moral Equivalent of War," did not in fact appear until 1910, three years after the publication of *Newer Ideals of Peace*, but the passage Addams quoted had actually appeared in 1902 in

James's *The Varieties of Religious Experience.* There he added: "I have often thought that in the old monkish poverty-worship . . . there might be something like that moral equivalent of war we are seeking."[30]

Addams herself had been writing and speaking on the theme of moral substitutes for war since at least 1899. At that time, without using the phrase itself, she said in her speech on "Democracy or Militarism" at the Chicago Liberty Meeting: "Let us not make the mistake of confusing moral issues sometimes involved in warfare with warfare itself. . . . The same strenuous endeavor, the same heroic self-sacrifice, the same fine courage and readiness to meet death, may be displayed without the accompaniment of killing our fellow men."[31]

In the spring of 1903, at Chicago's Ethical Culture Society, Addams introduced the phrase itself as the title of her talk on "A Moral Substitute for War." The following year, at the Universal Peace Congress in Boston, on October 5, 1904, she addressed the subject again at a women's meeting and then immediately afterward at a workingmen's public meeting: "We have been saying, over in the women's meeting . . . that [it] is incumbent on this generation . . . to discover a moral substitute for war, something that will appeal to the courage, the capacity of men, something which will develop their finest powers without deteriorating their moral nature, as war constantly does."[32]

Here she brought in another theme central to her ideas in *Newer Ideals of Peace,* the role of labor in relation to peace: "the only visible beginning which we can find for a moral substitute for war, is to be found in the labor movement as it is developing in every land on the face of the earth."[33] As in her address on "Democracy or Militarism" five years earlier, she again cited the International Association of Workingmen, founded in 1864, as "the first people to conceive the need of modern internationalism" to overcome the heavy burden of war on the workers: "Who should band together for preserving human life, for keeping the fields free from the tramping of soldiers, from the destruction of the precious bread that men love to have? I say it is the workers, who year after year nourish and bring up the bulk of the nation. . . . The peace movement should be in the hands of those who produce, and not be allowed to fall into the hands of those who destroy."[34]

Addams elaborated further on the "moral substitute" idea two days later at the banquet of the 1904 Peace Congress (at which James followed her on the program), suggesting that "the international man" should be told "that adventure is not only to be found in going forth into new lands and shooting; that youth and spirit can find other outlets; that we might make clear to him the pleasures that lie in the human spirit." She called up an image of "the excitement and the pleasure and the infinite moral stimulus and the gratification of the spirit of adventure to be found in the nourishing of human life."[35]

Addams now alluded to the manifestations of community mutual aid that came to figure prominently in *Newer Ideals of Peace.* "I said the other night at the Labor meeting that the only place where we saw the rising feeling which was going to sweep war from the face of the earth was in the organization of working men; but I have thought of a good many things since." Among these, she mentioned in particular the immigrant benefit societies which had "made a little wall between themselves and starvation and a pauper's grave. . . . It is in this direction, I believe, that much of our hope lies."[36]

Two years later, in *Newer Ideals of Peace,* as she carried further the discussion of moral substitutes for war, Addams turned more directly to examples at the international level, describing a new heroism "which pertains to labor and the nourishing of human life . . . [and] manifests itself at the present moment in a universal determination to abolish poverty and disease." Here she called up the massive campaign to eradicate tuberculosis, affording many examples of heroic effort and international cooperation, and the growing trend to provide for "neglected old age" through government pension plans and mutual benefit societies in various countries (pp. 16–17). In general terms, she characterized such efforts as the "newer humanitarianism" and the "substitution of nurture for warfare" (p. 17).

Thus among the primary features of this "newer humanitarianism" projected by Addams as "moral substitutes for war" were internationalism and collective action directed to improve social conditions and human welfare across bounds of class, race, ethnicity, geography, and other divisions. Though Addams supported and advocated efforts to strengthen the legal foundations for reaching these goals by combining common law and international law (p. 9), it was not necessarily through international *institutions* that this was to be achieved. Rather, Addams saw the dynamic processes of peaceful change as emerging from "the poorer quarters of a cosmopolitan city" (pp. 9–10). Though she was well aware of the vulnerability of the populace to jingoistic appeals and battle cries, and having herself pointed out that they might not always exhibit justice and righteousness, Addams's observations of life in the cosmopolitan city had led her to the conviction that the mass of ordinary people are more inclined to pursue peaceful and cooperative endeavors in their daily lives and treat each other with kindliness and compassion even across national, ethnic and class divisions (see section VI below).

On the same platform from which Addams addressed the Peace Congress in 1904, William James presented a fundamentally contrary view.[37] Though James later characterized himself as a "pacificist" and urged war prevention, his approach was grounded on his assertions that "our permanent enemy is the rooted bellicosity of human nature," and that "the plain truth is that people want war."[38] He pointed to what he claimed to be widespread approval and idealization of war throughout history and suggested that war must inspire "some awe, in spite of all the horrors." Moreover, "A deadly listlessness would come over most men's imagination of the future if they could seriously be brought to believe that never again . . . would a war trouble human history. In such a stagnant summer afternoon of a world, where would be the zest or interest?"[39] His pragmatic solution was to "go in for preventive medicine, not for radical cure," and his initial short list of suggested actions included the election of "peace men," education, and use of arbitration. James did not use the phrase "moral equivalent of war" in this speech, and his sole reference to substitutes for war was a recommendation that we "foster rival excitements, and invent new outlets for heroic energy."

While fostering "rival" excitements was not exactly what Addams had in mind, she had indeed been talking about "new outlets for heroic energy" for some years past, and developed this idea more fully in 1906 in *Newer Ideals of Peace*. The kind of heroism she had in mind required, she wrote there, "a new and beneficent courage, an invincible ardor for conserving and healing human life, for understanding and elaborating it" (p. 118).

When James later expanded on his recommendation in his 1910 essay, "The Moral Equivalent of War, "he did so along lines that differed greatly from Addams's views, and indeed conflicted directly with her "newer ideals" of peace, accepting and even lauding the military virtues as essential to society. Despite his laudatory letter to her in 1907, stating that he found it "hard to express the good [the book] has done me in opening new points of view and annihilating old ones,"[40] he hardly seems to have taken in her main points—above all, the need to *overcome* the pervasive influence of the military virtues in society, and to recognize the central role of the city poor, the workers, youth, women, and "the unsuccessful" in achieving that goal.

James avoided Addams's plural term, "moral substitutes for war," in favor of a singular, more simplistic but perhaps more rhetorically persuasive phrase, "the moral equivalent of war"—a term he likened to "the mechanical equivalent of heat." In 1902 and 1904 he offered several brief suggestions of moral equivalents for war, but in his 1910 essay the central idea, which he characterized as a "utopian" and "socialistic" suggestion, was to substitute for military conscription "a conscription of the whole youthful population to form for a certain number of years a part of the army enlisted against *Nature*."[41] Thereby, he asserted: "The military ideals of hardihood and discipline would be wrought into the growing fibre of the people."

James followed this with a vision that bears careful examination. If his proposal were adopted, he wrote, "no one would remain blind as the luxurious classes now are blind, to man's relations to the globe he lives on, and to the permanently sour and hard foundations of his higher life":

> To coal and iron mines, to freight trains, to fishing fleets in December, to dishwashing, clothes-washing, and window-washing, to road-building and tunnel-making, to foundries and stoke-holes, and to the frames of skyscrapers, would our gilded youths be drafted off, according to their choice, to get the childishness knocked out of them, and to come back into society with healthier sympathies and soberer ideas. They would . . . tread the earth more proudly, the women would value them more highly, they would be better fathers and teachers of the following generation. . . .[42]

James was confident that men were capable of organizing such a system of national service as a moral equivalent of war, "or some other just as effective for preserving manliness of type."

Though James framed his proposal as a conscription of "the whole youthful population" (a fine example of the false universal as analyzed recently by Hilda Smith[43]), it is evident that he had in mind only males (note "the women would value them more highly"). Moreover, his proposal was clearly directed to the "gilded youth" of the upper classes, since the youth of the working classes already had more than enough experience of having "the childishness knocked out of them" by hard labor.

James did not elaborate on why he thought this short-term participation by (elite) young men in an alternative "army against nature"—a notion that would hardly be thought of as consistent with positive peace today—would still their "rooted bellicosity" or provide "outlets for heroic energy" for the rest of their lives. Nor did he explain how these activities by a small segment of the population would satisfy the need for "rival excitements" in the rest of the population any better than would the same activities carried out by workers in the ordinary course of making a living, nor why those who engaged in these activities daily over their lifetimes might still rally to the call to war when summoned.

Addams did at times frame the problem of "moral substitutes" as a search for alternative means of meeting certain general social-psychological needs that had been traditionally met through war. For example, she wrote: "Warfare in the past has done much to bring men together. A sense of common danger and the stirring appeal to action for a common purpose, easily open the channels of sympathy through which we partake of the life about us." However, she followed this immediately with the remark that "there are certainly other methods of opening those channels" (p. 118).

Similarly, wherever Addams acknowledged a useful role of warfare in the past, it was always with disclaimers suggesting that there were other—better—ways to achieve those purposes, or purposes more suited to new social conditions. "Let us by all means acknowledge and preserve that which has been good in warfare and in the spirit of warfare; let us gather it together and incorporate it in our national fibre," she wrote (p. 117). But she followed this with the remark that "war is an implement too clumsy and barbaric to subserve our purposes" (p. 118), and went on to argue strongly, "The task that is really before us is first to see to it, that the old virtues bequeathed by war are not retained after they have become a social deterrent and that social progress is not checked by a certain contempt for human nature which is but the inherited result of conquest"(p. 118).

At heart, though Addams and James were both speaking of "moral substitutes" or "moral equivalents" for war, they were actually working within sharply different paradigms. Addams's approach was internationalist, not only in principle but in the very details of the moral substitutes she suggested, most requiring some form of international or interethnic cooperation. James, on the other hand, posed a national-service model without reference to such cooperation. Linda Schott has reviewed numerous other differences between them—regarding their views on human nature, appropriate sex roles, the need to preserve military values, and other matters. As Schott summed it up, "James' 'moral equivalent'. . . was designed to maintain a society dominated by wealthy men . . . in which women stayed in the private sphere and the poor went unnoticed. . . . Addams' 'moral substitute'. . . lauded the work of women and the poor and asked the traditional leaders of society to renounce competition, militarism, and war and experience the pleasure that came from nurturing others."[44]

Addams herself included several remarks that might well be taken as direct repudiations of James's argument. Where James's essay prescribed in 1910 that "the military ideals of hardihood and discipline would be wrought into the growing fibre of the people," Addams, in *Newer Ideals of Peace*, had scoffed at adherents of war for proclaiming "that it is interwoven with every fibre of human growth and is at the root of all that is noble and courageous in human life" (p. 117). To insist that the "pluck and energy" once elicited by war should continue to be expressed in the same form "would be as stupid a mistake as if we would relegate the full-grown citizen, responding to many claims and demands upon his powers, to the school-yard fights of his boyhood." For the adult citizen to carry over "those puerile instincts into manhood," she thought, would not show heroism but rather "arrested development" (p. 117).

Thus, despite the fact that they sometimes shared the same platforms, and despite the appearance of mutually high regard between Addams and James, it is hard to see how Addams can be imagined to have approved James's "moral equivalent of war," with its effusive praise of the military virtues and its rousing call to emulate them in civilian endeavors. In light of the marked theoretical and ideological differences between them, coupled with Addams's distinctive and independent search for "moral substitutes for war," it seems peculiar and regrettable that some of her biographers and reviewers chose James's phrase "moral equivalent" to characterize her idea, submerging or even erasing it beneath his.[45]

In her search for moral substitutes for war, Addams began to develop ideas of positive peace that have widespread resonance today.

VI. The Conceptualization of Positive Peace
in Newer Ideals of Peace

Addams acknowledged that "it is difficult to formulate the newer dynamic peace, embodying the later humanism, as over against the old dogmatic peace" (p. 7). Though she admired the "nonresistant strike" of the Russian peasantry against military conscription (p. 128), she rejected the word "nonresistance" as misleading, "feeble and inadequate," suggesting passivity and ineffectiveness (p. 7). In its place she suggested that "The words 'overcoming,' 'substituting,' 're-creating,' 'readjusting moral values,' 'forming new centres of spiritual energy' carry much more of the meaning implied" (pp. 7–8). These terms conveyed her sense that peace was a complex, dynamic process, not a static condition, "permanent" or "eternal."

In an important but little noted passage in her concluding chapter, "The Passing of the War Virtues," Addams argued that it was necessary "to distinguish between a social order founded upon law enforced by authority and that other social order which includes liberty of individual action and complexity of group development. The latter social order would not suppress the least germ of promise, of growth and variety, but would nurture all into a full and varied life" (p. 118). Addams thus challenged a commonly accepted image of peaceful society as defined by "law and order," setting it against a very different vision of a society encompassing both individual liberty and "complexity of group development." Rather than direct its resources to rewarding success and fostering elites, a peaceful society would "nurture all into a full and varied life."[46]

Addams did not believe there was a simple set of "substitutes for the war virtues." Rather, what was necessary was to determine the methods of *finding* them: "We come at last to the practical question as to how these substitutes for the war virtues may be found" (p. 120). Her general answer to this was that "*spontaneous and fraternal action* as virile and widespread as war itself is the only *method* by which substitutes for the war virtues may be *discovered*" (p. 118, emphasis added). But while this suggested a long-range process of change, carried out by many people over time, and therefore not predictable in its outcome, Addams did outline in *Newer Ideals of Peace* some of the characteristics and principles of that "other social order" corresponding to the "newer ideals of peace."

At the outset, we can discern in her critique of the founders that she envisioned "a type of government founded upon peace and fellowship as contrasted with restraint and defence" (p. 19). The details of this form of government would have to be worked out in a process encouraging free expression of the popular will, not reversion "to the military and legal type" (p. 22) nor resort to "penalties, coercion, compulsion, remnants of military codes, to hold the community together" (p. 21).

This process would require reform or reconstitution of the machinery of government by which the founders had "carefully defined what was germane to government and what was quite outside its realm," and instead accept that "the very crux of local self-government, as has been well said, is involved in the 'right to locally determine the scope of the local government,' in response to needs as they arise" (p. 22).

Although Addams did not have full confidence that a "democratic" public would necessarily be opposed to war, she nevertheless held that it would not do to "keep the reins of government in the hands of the good and professedly public-spirited" (p. 22), and that to move in the direction of the newer ideals of peace it was necessary to start from the bottom, trusting the complex processes of local self-government to deal with the real problems and needs of the community.

Addams compared American city governance unfavorably with European counterparts she found closer to her ideas: "London has twenty-eight Borough Councils, in addition to the London County Council itself, fifteen hundred direct representatives of the people, as over against seventy in Chicago although the latter has a population one-half as large. Paris has twenty Mayors, with corresponding machinery for local government, as over against the New York concentration in one huge City Hall, too often corrupt" (pp. 49–50). Clearly she favored breaking down massive concentrations of people into smaller self-governing units in which the people would have more voice and scope for their own initiative, and more direct control over their representatives and machinery of government.

This was based on Addams's conviction that constructive substitutes for the war virtues would emerge from "the poorer quarters of [the] cosmopolitan city." Despite the terrible pressures on the poor, and the "ruthlessness" (p. 10) prevalent in their lives, "certain it is," she wrote, "that these quarters continually confound us by their manifestations of altruism" (p. 13). This should not be so surprising, she argued, once it is recognized that under such conditions it is essential to live one's life "with some reference to the demands of social justice" in order to avoid both crushing others and being crushed oneself (p. 13). "We are often told," she wrote, "that men under this pressure of life become calloused and cynical, whereas anyone who lives with them knows that they are sentimental and compassionate" (p. 13).

Thus from direct observation, Addams concluded that the cosmopolitan neighborhoods of the poor would produce an "irresistible coalescing of the altruistic and egoistic impulse" (p. 13) which she thought to be "the strength of social morality" and the foundation of that "cosmopolitan affection" emerging in the large cities (p. 9): "In seeking companionship in the new world, all the immigrants are reduced to the fundamental equalities and universal necessities of human life itself, and they inevitably develop the power of association which comes from daily contact with those who are unlike each other in all save the universal characteristics of man" (p. 11). Yet Addams recognized that social sympathy alone would not suffice: "the social sentiments are as blind as the egoistic sentiments and must be enlightened, disciplined and directed by the fullest knowledge" (p. 9).

Production and dissemination of this necessary knowledge was in large measure the task Addams and her associates at Hull-House had long set themselves, for example in *Hull-House Maps and Papers.*[47] This was the task Addams set for herself in the main body of *Newer Ideals of Peace,* with its attention to a multitude of issues and examples in the daily life of the city. While she believed the "cosmopolitan affection" emerging among the poor in the cities was international in its implications—a "cosmopolitan humanitarianism ignoring national differences" (p. 43)—it was in resolving the conflicts and transcending the militarist habits of daily life and work that she saw the evolution of the "newer ideals of peace."

In the central chapters of the book, therefore, she turned to specific issues and recommendations of policy to promote that evolution, towards what we would certainly today call positive peace, a peace grounded in social justice and social welfare. She denounced in detail "the exploitation and industrial debasement of the immigrant" (pp. 26–28) and argued that municipal government must concern itself with "the social needs of the people" (p. 31).

Unfortunately, she thought, American political leaders were mired in the restricted and outmoded model of coercive government handed down by its military inheritance, which admitted only the most limited responsibility for the welfare of the populace.

On that outdated theory of government, she contended, American governments declined assistance to the *working* poor. Even in dealing with adult prisoners, she noted, the civil governments, "while continuing to maintain prisons, have become more or less ashamed of them, and are already experimenting in better ways to elevate and reform criminals than by the way of violence and imprisonment." But in dealing with an ordinary worker in stringent circumstances, "if he is turned away from the hospital without tuberculosis, merely too depleted and wretched to go back to his regular employment, then the city can do nothing for him unless he be ready to call himself an out-and-out pauper" (pp. 47–48). The central problem, she argued, was that "[w]e are afraid of the notion of governmental function which would minister to the primitive needs of the mass of the people" (p. 48). Addams tied this to a problem of democratic governance all too present to us today, the disinterest of large numbers of the working classes in the electoral process. "It is really the rank and file, the average citizen, who is ignored by the government, while he works out his real problems through other agencies, although he is scolded for staying at home on election day" (p. 48).

In the interest of strengthening a government which would "minister to the primitive needs of the mass of the people," Addams set aside her reservations about systems of coercive law, which she saw as generally serving the interests of the rich and refusing responsibility for the needs of the poor, in favor of strict regulation of economic and industrial forces to control abuse, exploitation, and degradation of both people and the environment: "We need rigid enforcement of the existing laws, while at the same time, we frankly admit the inadequacy of these laws, and work without stint for progressive regulations better fitted to the newer issues among which our lot is cast; for, unless the growing conscience is successfully embodied in legal enactment, men lose the habit of turning to the law for guidance and redress" (p. 66).

Along these lines, Addams called for "the enforcement of adequate child labor laws" as well as compulsory education, expressing her admiration for the immigrant mothers "who wash and scrub for the meagre support of their children" so that they can attend school rather than go to work to relieve some of the burden on their parents (p. 42). On the other hand, she faulted the harsh and arbitrary treatment in the criminal courts of youths arrested, often for petty crimes, and argued for education rather than punishment for juvenile offenders and poor immigrant children (pp. 45–47). She commended the commitment of American governments to public education, remarking that "public education has long been a passion in America, and we seem to have been willing to make that an exception to our general theory of government" (p. 48); that is, the restricted view of government derived from the military heritage.

Addams blamed the same military inheritance for the implicit or explicit contempt for immigrants prevalent in the attitudes of both reformers and corrupt politicians: "this attitude of contempt, of provincialism, this survival of the spirit of the conqueror toward an inferior people" (p. 29). She offered an unusual analysis of the paradoxical situation of police, called upon to carry out "repressive legislation, the remnant of a military state of society" against members of their own communities (p. 32).

Against this attitude of contempt, Addams argued for recognition of the self-governing traditions and productive skills of immigrant groups having experience of alternative systems of village organization, land tenure, and taxation (pp. 37–39). She was particularly interested in "those early organizations of village communities, folk-motes, and mirs, those primary cells of both industrial and political organizations, where the people knew no difference between the two, but, quite simply, met to consider in common discussion all that concerned their common life" (p. 67).[48] Studies of such village communities, she suggested, might offer models and resources for viable forms of self-governance at the local level, and for what we today would call participatory democracy in other contexts. She also found promise in attention to the history and survivals of medieval "crafts, guilds, and artels, which combine government with daily occupations, as did the self-governing university and free town" (p. 67).

Addams drew from the example of the art and architecture of the Middle Ages for an alternative to the notion that great achievements required a system of individualism and competition. Rather, she suggested, one should "seek for the connection between the liberty-loving mediaeval city and its free creative architecture, that art which combines the greatest variety of artists and artisans" (p. 67). As she had noted earlier:

> The Gothic cathedrals were glorious beyond the dreams of artists, notwithstanding that they were built by unknown men, or rather by so many men that it was a matter of indifference to record their names. . . . The old cathedral-builders fearlessly portrayed all of life, its inveterate tendency to deride as well as to bless, its trickery as well as its beauty. (p. 15)

Meditating on the extraordinary beauty, majesty, and humanity of the cathedrals built by these unknowns, however, Addams was moved to unfavorable comparisons with the culture of her own time. She feared that even humanitarian efforts in the twentieth century were in danger of going awry. In yet another painfully prescient warning that would be well for us to heed in the twenty-first century, she wrote: "Could we compare the present humanitarian efforts to the building of a spiritual cathedral, it would seem that the gargoyles had been made first, that the ground is now strewn with efforts to 'do good' which have developed a diabolical capacity for doing harm" (p. 15).

This fear reveals a deep strain of pessimism seldom recognized in Addams. But it was consistent with her distrust of success and of even the most well-meaning elite leadership. Addams believed it was necessary to turn to "the unsuccessful" for the source of humanitarian internationalism. She wrote in *Newer Ideals of Peace,* in a remarkable passage seldom noted:

That 'ancient kindliness which sat beside the cradle of the race,' and which is ever ready to assert itself against ambition and greed and the desire for achievement, is manifesting itself now with unusual force, and for the first time presents international aspects. (p. 8)[49]

What is remarkable here is the coupling of "ambition" and even "desire for achievement" with "greed" as harmful motives in government and international affairs. Indeed, Addams argued that "emotional pity and kindness are always found in greatest degree among the unsuccessful" and suggested that it was "among the huge mass of the unsuccessful, to be found in certain quarters of the modern city," from which the "first growth of the new compassion" would develop (p. 10).

Addams saw this not merely as an article of faith in the ideals of the humble, "which all religious teachers unite in declaring to be the foundations of a sincere moral life" (p. 18), but as a practical political reality. "If successful struggle ends in blatant and tangible success for the few only, government will have to reckon most largely with the men who have been beaten in the struggle, with the effect upon them of the contest and the defeat; for, after all, the unsuccessful will always represent the majority of the citizens, and it is with the large majority that self-government must eventually deal" (p. 36).

Here Addams returned to the central theme already noted: the need for government to concern itself with human needs. Thus she gave extensive attention in *Newer Ideals of Peace* to the pressing issues of immigrant life, child labor, the factory system, unions, strikes, women workers, protective legislation, denial of the franchise to women, crime, corrupt politicians, misguided reformers, police, public safety and sanitation, environmental conditions of work and city life, and a host of other specific problems of daily existence and struggle under the "new and strenuous conditions" of her time. Though some reviewers saw these concerns as diverging from "the peace issue," as it had been understood for the most part in the peace movements of the past, Addams was explicit in arguing that these were at the heart of the "newer ideals" that must be pursued if society were to arrive at a condition of positive peace, both at home and abroad.

Moreover, as we have seen, Addams was equally concerned with the process by which these ideals might be pursued. She challenged the view, still predominant today, that improvement in the conditions of life of the poorest communities "must largely come from forces outside the life of the people" (p. 49), that is from educators, business interests, and philanthropists. She posed instead a set of incisive questions: "What vehicle of correction is provided for the people themselves, what device has been invented for loosing that kindliness and mutual aid which is the marvel of all charity visitors? What broad basis has been laid down for a modification of their most genuine and pressing needs through their own initiative?" (p. 49).

Addams applied the same principle to her analysis of the status and roles of women. Denied the franchise on the basis of an outmoded militarist idea that "the ultimate value of the elector could be reduced to his ability to perform military duty" (p. 100), she argued, women were thus also denied a voice in control over the radically changed conditions of their lives and work under industrial capitalism. Citing data on the increasing percentages of women in the industrial work force, and especially the large percentage of young women sixteen to twenty years old, Addams called for "uniform and enforceable statutes" to protect the health and safety of workers against speed-ups in the factories and sweatshops, as well as conditions in dangerous employments. "The injurious effects of employments involving the use of poisons, acids, gases, atmospheric extremes, or other dangerous processes," she wrote, "still await adequate investigation and legislation in this country" (pp. 105–6). And, she asked, "How shall this take place save by the concerted efforts of the women themselves, those who are employed, and those other women who are intelligent as to the worker's needs and who possess a conscience in regard to industrial affairs?" (p. 106).

Addams's wording here is worthy of note, in regard to the reproach that she was "essentialist" in her view of women. It is clear that she did not see "women" in general as necessarily advocating such health and safety measures, but explicitly specified the need for involvement of working women themselves and those women "who are intelligent as to the worker's needs and who possess a conscience in regard to industrial affairs." By "intelligent," Addams did not mean educated elite women, but rather those who, though not workers themselves, were well informed and perceptive concerning working women's issues.

As she made clear repeatedly throughout the book, she did not see education or learning in themselves as guarantees of good conscience or good policies. She was skeptical of the nature and content of prevailing trends in education. Thus with regard to woman suffrage, Addams rejected the view that it "would be valuable only so far as the educated women exercised it. . . . Those matters in which woman's judgment is most needed," she argued, "are far too primitive and basic to be largely influenced by what we call education" (p. 104). What was necessary was a different kind of knowledge, for example, investigative knowledge of the "sanitary condition of all the factories and workshops . . . in which the industrial processes are at present carried on in great cities, intimately affect[ing] the health and lives of thousands of workingwomen" (p. 104).

Addams was deeply concerned with changes in the status and terms of women's work in modern industry, in which women continued to do all the kinds of work which had been done by their grandmothers: "the spinning, dyeing, weaving, and sewing. . . . the brewing and baking and thousands of operations which have been pushed out of the domestic system into the factory system." But now they found themselves at work in the factories or sweatshops, or lacking the resources to carry on their work as before, and "surrounded by conditions over which they have no control" (p. 104). She saw these changes as intensifying women's need for participation in public life: "Women directly controlled the surroundings of their work as long as their arrangements were domestic, but they cannot do this now unless they have the franchise" (p. 106).

As we have seen, Addams associated self-governance with an expanding recognition of social needs as an appropriate focus of government action. In Germany, however, she found an evolution in which it was not so much local self-governance as popular pressure from the Social Democratic party which brought the central government "to concern itself with the primitive essential needs of its working-people" (p. 50). She was impressed with Germany's system of social insurance, taxing large manufacturers to underwrite accident and health insurance and old-age pensions, and where proposals were under consideration for unemployment insurance and rent control (p. 50).

Addams was also struck by the transformation of German police forces into agencies of record and local enforcement of regulations concerning transportation; forests; vaccinations; inspections of meat, food, and factories; and other functions of the social service system (pp. 50–51). She suggested that this extension of function had "broken down the military ideal in the country where that ideal is most firmly intrenched" (p. 51). That the entrenched military ideal might ultimately overturn the balance through catastrophic events such as the world wars and the Nazi rise to power was a prospect that might not have come as a total surprise to Addams, but at the time this was written, the transformation of police forces to positive and constructive functions in serving the needs of the people was a model she regarded as hopeful. It is surprising that she failed to recognize the dangers of entrusting such functions to the police, an inherently military institution, but she found only the negative in the American model (p. 51).

In developing her conceptions of positive peace, Addams drew on the ideas and projects of socialism, even those of German Social Democracy, which was grounded in Marxism. But she rejected any form of dogmatism, and had reservations about socialism on that ground: "The surprising growth of Socialism, at the moment, is due largely to the fact that it is the only political party upon an international basis, and also that it frankly ventures its future upon a better industrial organization. These two aspects have had much more to do with its hold in industrial neighborhoods than have its philosophic tenets or the impassioned appeal of its propagandists" (p. 63).

Though Addams saw the socialists as the only political force pressing for that expansion of government she sought, to "extend its kindliness to the normal working man," she faulted them for adopting the same kind of abstract dogma as did other ideologists: "They refuse . . . to deal with the present State and constantly take refuge in the formulae of a new scholasticism. Their orators are busily engaged in establishing two substitutes for human nature which they call 'proletarian' and 'capitalist'" (p. 48). But Addams did not mean to set a uniform or essentialist "human nature" in opposition to the class analysis of the socialists. Rather, it was the essentialist and dichotomous character of the "two substitutes" to which she took exception:

> They ignore the fact that varying, imperfect human nature is incalculable, and that to eliminate its varied and constantly changing elements is to face all the mistakes and miscalculations which gath-

ered around the "fallen man," or the "economic man," or any other of the fixed norms which have from time to time been substituted for expanding and developing human life. In time "the proletarian" and "the capitalist" will become the impedimenta which it will be necessary to clear away in order to make room for the mass of living and breathing citizens with whom self-government must eventually deal. (pp. 48–49)

Addams's newer ideals of peace thus encompassed a broad range of concerns that have come to be identified with ideas of positive peace today, particularly in regard to social welfare, economic justice, gender roles, and participatory democracy. That our current issues, language, and priorities may differ in some respects from hers should be no surprise (for example in her common use of the false universal "man"), but there are disquieting remarks and silences in *Newer Ideals of Peace*, especially around race issues, that call for further consideration.

VII. Questions of "Race"

Addams has been faulted for certain ethnocentric and sexist assumptions in her writings, and instances of this may be found in *Newer Ideals of Peace*. For the most part, these take the form of passing remarks or significant omissions which betray the fact that, despite her explicit rejection of attitudes of superiority and dominance, her ideas were still influenced by prevailing stereotypes and misconceptions. Thus she mentioned in passing "the freeing of the Christians from the oppressions of the Turks, of the Spaniards from the Moslems" (p. 125) with apparently no awareness of the historical complexities of relations between Christians and Muslims. Though Addams often used the terms "savage" and "primitive" to refer to traits and behaviors she admired, such as compassion and cooperation, or the ancient indigenous arts of conquered peoples, in some cases her use of these terms reflected attitudes not far removed from the imperialist arrogance she elsewhere decried. In arguing that the lure of war takes "young men" (i.e., white Western middle-class men) into militarist paths abroad, she wrote: "It incites their ambitions, not to irrigate, to make fertile and sanitary, the barren plain of the savage, but to fill it with military posts and tax-gatherers, to cease from pushing forward industrial action into new fields and to fall back upon military action" (p. 121). Despite the rejection here of a policy of conquest by military action and the imposition of "military posts and tax-gatherers," Addams put forward at the same time the neoimperialist idea, still widespread today, that "industrial action" should "make fertile and sanitary the barren plain of the savage."

Similarly, in a passage concerning labor unions and strikes, Addams reflected on the growing cooperation between union workers and "immigrants." She acknowledged in passing "that the trades union record on Chinese exclusion and negro [sic] discrimination has been damaging" (p. 53). Nevertheless, she went on at some length to describe and express admiration for the fact that the "assimilation between the immigrant and the workingman has exhibited amazing strength." Obviously "the immigrant" here is not meant to include Chinese immigrants, and "the workingman" is not meant to include either Chinese or Negro workers. In the same passage, Addams blamed employers for "the importation of immigrants as a wage-lowering weapon," calling it "the under-cutting of wages by the lowering of racial standard" (p. 54).

What she meant by "the lowering of racial standard" is difficult to discern. The term "racial" here is not used to designate racial groups as we would understand them today. Addams used the term "race" throughout *Newer Ideals of Peace* in a broadly fluid way, sometimes to designate any ethnic or national population, sometimes all of humanity ("the human race"). This was quite common usage in her time. For example, she cited a study of the 1904 Chicago stockyards strike by John R. Commons of the University of Wisconsin. Commons had described this as a strike of "Americanized Irish, Germans, and Bohemians, in behalf of Slovaks, Poles, and Lithuanians," and remarked that "this substitution of races in the stock yards has been a continuing process for twenty years" (p. 54). Though Addams was also conscious of the intensification of "race animosity" towards blacks that might develop during a strike, she saw it as only one variety of racist feeling. Discussing the Teamsters' strike of 1905, she wrote: "there is an enormous increase in the feeling of race animosity, beginning with the imported negro strike-breakers, and easily extending to 'Dagoes' and all other distinct nationalities" (p. 78).

Undoubtedly her remark about "lowering the racial standard" was intended to describe the employers' tactic of bringing in vulnerable new groups to replace workers in an established labor force, either to break a strike or simply to drive down wages. But to use the phrase without critical comment seems inconsistent with Addams's rejection of imperial attitudes of contempt for oppressed groups. As we have seen, Addams was conscious not only of abuses, problems, and conflicts experienced by immigrants from diverse ethnic and national backgrounds, but also of the cultural gifts and political alternatives they brought to American society. She urged the need to recognize the "political ideals of the Celtic, Germanic, Latin, and Slavic immigrants who have successively come to us," and "to work out a democratic government which should include the experiences and hopes of all the varied peoples among us" (pp. 28–29). As this passage suggests, however, her vision of "all the varied people among us" appears to have been limited here primarily to immigrants of European descent. She dealt very little in *Newer Ideals of Peace* with either the problems or the contributions of such "varied peoples" as African, Asian, and Latin American immigrants, or Native American Indians.

These omissions are puzzling, particularly as concerns African Americans, since Addams had been a prominent supporter of African American efforts for race equality. She herself made reference to the influence of "my Abolitionist father" in dealing with race issues in later life,[50] and she was certainly opposed to race prejudice and discrimination in her conscious views and in many actions. In February 1909, Addams was one of sixty prominent Americans who signed the call to a national conference which led to the founding of the National Association for the Advancement of Colored People (NAACP); she served for several years as a member of its executive committee.[51] She gave positive support to African American women leaders such as Mary Church Terrell and Ida B. Wells-Barnett. Wells-Barnett had found Addams actively responsive to calls for assistance (for example in stopping a move to segregate the Chicago public schools), and wrote in her memoirs that she regarded Addams as "the greatest woman in the United States."[52] Addams invited leaders of the colored women's clubs to a luncheon at Hull-House in 1899, an action significant enough to create a stir in the press at the time.[53] In 1901 she published an article in the *Indepen-*

dent protesting lynching.[54] She was a supporter of W. E. B. DuBois and invited him, as well as other black leaders, to speak at Hull-House.[55] In 1912, she fought a bitter but unsuccessful battle in the Progressive Party to seat black delegates, and published an article discussing the issues in the *Crisis,* the magazine of the NAACP.[56] In 1915 she gave an interview to the *New York Evening Post* strongly condemning the racist messages in D. W. Griffith's film *Birth of a Nation.*[57] In 1919, she included Terrell, president of the National Association of Colored Women, among the U.S. delegates to the Zurich Congress of the International Committee of Women for Permanent Peace, and supported Terrell's proposal for a resolution on "Race Equality" that was adopted by the congress, over the opposition of other white women who wanted weaker wording.[58]

There were certainly limitations in Addams's understanding of racism, and this has been noted by a number of critics. Yet it is ironic that the most intense scrutiny has been addressed to what may have been her most controversial and courageous efforts, namely, her anti-lynching article of January 1901 in the *Independent* and her single-handed campaign to seat black delegates at the 1912 Progressive Party convention.

As to the first, Ida B. Wells-Barnett had responded to Addams in the same journal in May 1901. Wells-Barnett identified a number of racist assumptions that marred what Addams had written on lynching, and marshaled statistics and factual details to refute the egregious stereotype of the black male rapist, to which Addams had unfortunately lent credence. Wells-Barnett had already impressively demonstrated in her previous publications that lynching was mainly about maintaining white political and economic dominance over the black population rather than protecting "white womanhood" from black male sexual assault.[59] Wells-Barnett's critique was lost to view for decades after, but in 1977 Bettina Aptheker expanded on these arguments and related issues in her introduction to *Lynching and Rape: An Exchange of Views,* in which she reprinted the exchange between Addams and Wells-Barnett.[60] Aptheker nevertheless concluded that "Wells' estimate of Jane Addams as an outstanding and courageous personality is eminently appropriate."[61] But Patricia A. Schechter, in *Ida B. Wells-Barnett and American Reform, 1880–1930,* has suggested a less favorable view: "white reformers like Addams resisted Wells-Barnett's arguments about lynching's deep causes."[62]

Perhaps it was because of this resistance that five years after the 1901 exchange, when Addams was writing *Newer Ideals of Peace,* she did not make the connection that might well have been made between Wells-Barnett's campaign against the violence of lynching and Addams's search for heroic "moral substitutes for war" and ways to achieve the goals of positive peace. But we should not be too smug in reproaching Addams for this omission, since to this day, Wells-Barnett and the anti-lynching movement have been almost totally ignored in histories of movements for peace and nonviolence, and in the field of peace studies at large.

At the time of the controversy over seating black delegates in 1912, Addams was bitterly reproached for continuing to support and campaign for Theodore Roosevelt and the Progressive Party even after their refusal to accept her resolution. Her article in the *Crisis* in 1912 was a defense of her actions, at the same time acknowledging her own doubts about her choices: "Was I more dissatisfied with this action than I had often been with no action at all?" But she was also led to reflect on some international implications of this struggle, which had come to underline for her, some six years after *Newer Ideals of Peace,* the importance of race issues on the international level: "In fact it has already been discovered at the Hague that many difficulties formerly called international were in reality interracial."[63]

VIII. Ambivalent Reception: Praise,
Neglect, Rediscovery

When first published, reported James Linn, *Newer Ideals of Peace* was "enthusiastically received," the reviewers "spoke in high praise of it," and it "became a best seller on the basis of its philosophy." One of the most admiring comments came in that private letter from William James, quoted above (pp. ix–x), but this was matched by some published reviews, such as that of a Hearst editor quoted by Linn: "On the whole the reach of this woman's sympathy and understanding is beyond all comparison wider in its span, comprehending more kinds of people, than that of any public man. And . . . this comprehension is not, in Miss Addams, purchased at the price of vagueness and sentimentality. She is a thinker and a woman of action. . . . To the dust-dry counsels of materialists and statisticians she brings the lift and passion of large ideas."[64]

Most of the reviews published in 1907 recognized that Addams's approach was significantly different from the prevailing analyses of the problems she discussed. They placed her outside the mainstream in various ways. The *American Monthly Review of Reviews* put it most succinctly: "a presentation of the peace argument from a wholly new point of view."[65] The *Annals of the American Academy of Political and Social Science* wrote of the "rare combination of power of insight and of interpretation" and the "fresh virile thought . . . which has characterized [Addams's] work."[66]

After a lengthy summary of the main ideas of the book, sociologist George Herbert Mead asserted: "Nowhere can one find the social point of view . . . presented with so much inherent necessity as here . . . not the necessity of a deduction, but the necessity of immediate reality . . . [which is] all the more impressive because our eyes have been holden from [it] by economic and political abstractions."[67] Olivia Howard Dunbar, writing in *North American Review*, emphasized Addams's "fresh and independent conclusions" and intellectual integrity: "It is her striking distinction that she does not feel bound to square her statements with empty academic formula [*sic*] nor to consider their bearing on her own political present or future."[68]

The *Literary Digest* pointed to the unique empirical basis of Addams's ideas: "The views of the author differ considerably from those of other writers on the subject and have been deeply influenced by the environment and conditions of settlement work in a great metropolitan city." Unlike the "academic views of the ordinary writer on sociology, they rest on a basis of reality and are qualified by actual experience and sympathy with the life of a widely assorted humanity." This reviewer also discerned the radicalism of Addams's approach: "A firm believer in the possibility of the establishment of world peace based upon the mutual consent and interest of the nations, Miss Addams differs radically from other well-known writers as to the means by which this ideal is to be realized. . . . The author thinks that . . . universal peace will be reached through the cooperation of those very elements who are now looked on as disturbers of order in the nation—the immigrant population."[69]

Reactions to *Newer Ideals of Peace* were not entirely positive, however. Theodore Roosevelt, in a private conversation with a friend of Jane Addams, said that "she has just written a bad book, a very bad book! She is all wrong about peace."[70] The pro-military perspectives she wrote against in the book were not, of course, suddenly demolished. For example, a Chicago newspaper argued that "as the world is now constituted circumstances may arise in which it is necessary for a nation to go to war and when not going to war is a national dishonor."[71]

More interesting are the critical comments from reviewers who were on the whole favorable toward the book but challenged some of Addams's assertions on substantive grounds. A case in point is a review in the *Advocate of Peace,* the journal of the American Peace Society, of which Addams was a vice president. The unsigned review (probably written by the editor, Benjamin Trueblood) considered two of her chapters (on "survivals of militarism in civil government" and "the passing of the war virtues") to be "very instructive," and the other chapters to be "strong, as studies of social conditions, though they deal less nearly with the question of peace." But the reviewer objected that Addams had failed to "do full justice to the older form of peace propaganda." Trueblood was evidently displeased by Addams's representation of the newer ideals as far different from those of earlier peace advocates, who had "never failed to point out the constructive measures necessary to secure and maintain peace, and laid strong emphasis at times on the social and industrial aspects of the question, as well as upon the great heroisms of common life furnishing an outlet to the pent-up energies of human nature."[72] This was indeed a valid claim, but Trueblood did not fully appreciate what was new in Addams's book. In judging that only two of the chapters of the book had direct bearing on "the question of peace," he revealed how little he understood her analysis of the pervasive militarization of social life, the links between social conditions and the search for peace, and her new conceptualization of "negative" and "positive" peace.

Another perspective came from the *Nation,* whose reviewer faulted Addams for failing to show exactly "how the evils on which she dwells are to be removed." In rejecting "the panacea of socialism," the reviewer argued, Addams failed to offer any "constructive programme" in its place, leaving "the tremendous problem of the relation of government to the mass . . . still unsolved."[73] Again, it appears that the reviewer had missed much of the content of the book, especially in its efforts to delineate the necessity of self-governance and decision making "from below" as central to "the relation of government to the mass" in a democratic society.

Newer Ideals of Peace was reprinted in 1911 and 1915, suggesting its continuing attraction for many readers, perhaps the more so in view of the war in progress in Europe and the hope of keeping the United States out of it. With the growing support and eventual commitment of the United States to the Allied side in the war, the messages of *Newer Ideals of Peace* may have been overwhelmed by the increasing horror and hopelessness of the war itself. After the war, Addams wrote *Peace and Bread in Time of War* (1922) in response to the changed situation, and *Newer Ideals of Peace* was for the most part lost to view in subsequent decades.[74] Yet its ideas undoubtedly germinated in the thought of Addams's admirers and disciples, in part through the distorted version of her call for moral substitutes for war put forward by William James and his followers, in part through the more compatible versions developed by herself and the women's peace movement.[75] John Dewey wrote, in his introduction to the 1945 edition of Addams's *Peace and Bread in Time of War,* that *Newer Ideals of Peace* should be given much of the credit for the change in attitude that gave the phrase "Peace Movement" a deepened significance at the time of his own writing:

> It used to stand for something which upon the whole was negative, for an attitude that made it easy to identify pacifism with passivism. A large measure of credit for producing this latter change must go to Jane Addams. In her book *The* [sic] *Newer Ideals of Peace,* published some years before the outbreak of World War One, she set forth aims and methods that are so intimately connected with *Peace and Bread* that the two books form a whole. The aims and methods set forth in both are of a kind that more than justify her in referring to them as "vital and dynamic."[76]

But it was only in the later decades of the twentieth century that Addams's contributions as an intellectual and a theorist came under examination again, with a strangely mixed evaluation.[77]

Merle Curti, the eminent historian of American intellectual history and the American peace movement, wrote four decades ago: "It is somewhat curious that in tributes to Jane Addams (1860–1935) occasioned by her centennial year, no serious consideration has been given to her place in American intellectual history. . . . But on re-reading her ten books it seems clear that if justice has been done her heart and her social vision, it has not been done her mind."[78] Curti offered several explanations for this fact, including the perceptive observations that Addams "did not in any of her writings systematically set forth her social ideas in a way to please the scholars nowadays who set great store on what is called intellectual sophistication" and that "certain critics, influenced by the stereotype of the sentimental do-gooder which was common among intellectuals, were close to condescension in their judgments of her." Yet Curti himself went far to justify and reinforce the neglect of Addams's mind by hastily assuring the reader: "It is not my purpose to try to elevate Jane Addams into a major figure in our intellectual life."[79]

This pattern of giving with one hand and taking away with the other has been evident in other treatments of Jane Addams's intellectual work as well. A few years after Curti wrote this, Christopher Lasch took up the challenge in his 1965 anthology, *The Social Thought of Jane Addams.* Leonard Levy, the editor of the series in which the volume appeared, wrote in the foreword: "Jane Addams was more than a practical activist, more than a great spirit. . . . She was a first-rate intellect who has not been accorded the place she deserves as one of our leading social critics."[80] Lasch himself wrote: "This anthology . . . shows [Addams] as theorist and intellectual—a thinker of originality and daring."[81] Yet Lasch was not without some responsibility for the failure to secure recognition of this point. To begin with, some critics have found his treatment of Addams marred by sexist preconceptions.[82] Moreover, Lasch did not do much to persuade the reader of his contention by any systematic review or critique of the body of Jane Addams's political and social thought, such as would identify clearly her place in the history of political theory.

Neither was that goal achieved by John Farrell in *Beloved Lady: A History of Jane Addams' Ideas on Reform and Peace.* Though Farrell's book is one of the most important sources for information and bibliography relating to Addams's writings and the development of her ideas, it is more an intellectual *biography* and a history of Addams's political and reform activities than a critical analysis of her works.[83] No more than Lasch did Farrell succeed in conveying a clear general perception of Addams's place in the history of political thought or peace theory.

In these 1960s efforts to secure recognition of Addams's intellectual work, Sondra Herman, in *Eleven Against War* (1969), offered the most comprehensive and incisive analysis of Addams's internationalist and pacifist ideas, framing them in relation to Addams's general political philosophy, to the history of internationalist thought, and to the contested issues of war and imperialism that had again become so urgent as that tumultuous decade drew to a close.[84] Yet Herman's serious and important exposition of Addams's ideas went almost unnoticed in subsequent Addams scholarship. The persistence of the old stereotypes was manifest in several subsequent works on Addams, published in the next decade, all of which follow the pattern of giving with one hand, taking away with the other. Even Ann Firor Scott's biography in *Notable American Women* (1971), though long and laudatory, describes Addams as a "settlement founder, social reformer, and peace worker," rather than as an intellectual. The final paragraph includes the judgment that Addams's "mind was not the skilled instrument of the scholar or the logician, but one of intuitive wisdom."[85]

Allen Davis's full-length biography, *American Heroine: The Life and Legend of Jane Addams* (1973), though thorough and serious, gave little attention to the intellectual component of Addams's life and often, when it did, with depreciatory remarks. Moreover, Davis's preface cast open doubt upon Lasch's evaluation, stating that while the development of Addams's thought was "part of the story," the focus of his book was not primarily an intellectual biography, since she was "always more important as a publicist and popularizer than as an original thinker."[86]

The practice of dual praise and disparagement was even better represented in Daniel Levine's biography, *Jane Addams and the Liberal Tradition* (1971). Levine actually gave more attention to the substance of Addams's ideas than did Davis, and he went so far as to say that Addams "developed an ideology and a program that constituted a fundamental challenge to the nation as she found it."[87] But the reader's attention to Addams's ideas is deflected by Levine's introduction, in which he could not forbear to repeat derisive remarks, and—more strongly than

Davis—discounted any originality in Addams's thought. In describing her as an intellectual, he offered the classic formulation concerning women as social theorists, conforming perfectly to stereotypic images: "Jane Addams was not an original thinker of major importance. One can find predecessors for almost every one of her ideas in the writings of English Fabians, German political economists, American pragmatists. Her importance was not as a manufacturer of ideas, but as their retailer."[88] One encounters almost identical remarks in many assessments of women's intellectual work. Wherever women have made a mark in social theory, it seems, it must be erased with the same ritual dismissal, expressed again and again in the very same words: "She was not an original thinker; her importance was as a popularizer or persuader."[89]

With regard to Addams, this evaluation has changed substantially in recent years with the appearance of new editions of her works and a number of important studies highlighting the intellectual work of women. One of the most important of these is Mary Jo Deegan's *Jane Addams and the Men of the Chicago School, 1892–1918*. Deegan presents Addams as "a major intellectual," "a force shaping American thought," and "a social theorist of major proportions." Deegan argues strongly that Addams's intellectual leadership has been obscured "because her most radical ideas are unpopular and she has been stigmatized by being reduced to an image of womanhood."[90] Though Deegan treats *Newer Ideals of Peace* very briefly, she offers an unusual interpretation of Addams's concept of peace as expressing "her vision of cultural feminism" (Deegan, 239). In contrast with Farrell's view of "pacifism as the underlying theme of all of Addams' work [after 1914]," Deegan argues that Addams's "cultural feminism embraced and explained pacifism," reaching "a clear exposition in her 1922 publication, *Peace and Bread in Time of War*" (Deegan, 240).

Two other recent works on women's contributions to the field of sociology give serious attention to Addams: *The Women Founders of the Social Sciences* by Lynn McDonald (1994), and *The Women Founders: Sociology and Social Theory, 1830–1930—A Text/Reader*, edited by Patricia Madoo Lengermann and Jill Niebrugge-Brantley (1998).[91] Lynn McDonald, arguing that women played a major role in the development of the social sciences, especially with regard to empirical methodology, focused primarily on Addams's "pioneering work in quantitative methods." Drawing on Deegan's analysis, McDonald notes particularly that in 1895 Addams and the women of Hull-House, in *Hull-House Maps and Papers,* had "published the first work of the 'Chicago School of Sociology,' giving it its defining characteristics: urban, problem-oriented, and quantitative," decades before the work of Ernest W. Burgess and Robert Park in the 1920s and 1930s. Lengermann and Niebrugge-Brantley, on the other hand, provide a broader treatment of Addams's ideas as a social theorist, and emphasize the feminist character of her methodology.

Jane Addams's social, political, and philosophical ideas have been addressed also by Charlene Seigfried in *Pragmatism and Feminism: Reweaving the Social Fabric,* and in Seigfried's introductions to two entries in the current series of University of Illinois reprint editions of Addams's works.[92] Jean Elshtain's *Jane Addams and the Dream of American Democracy* is noteworthy, though seriously distorted in its treatment of Addams's ideas on peace and war, as discussed below.[93] There are also a number of important articles, such as Linda Schott's "Jane Addams and William James on Alternatives to War."[94] New introductions to other reprint editions in the University of Illinois Press collection, and to the four-volume Thoemmes Press collection of Jane Addams's writings on peace, offer strong interpretations of the content of Addams's work. These recent works, taken together, open the way to a fuller and more just understanding of Addams's significance in American intellectual history.[95]

Nevertheless, in the field of peace studies, Addams is known primarily as an activist and social reformer.[96] Nowhere is she accorded recognition as a major peace theorist, or, in general, as an author of important writings on war and peace worthy of inclusion in anthologies of readings for peace studies classes. Thus Peter Mayer's *The Pacifist Conscience* (1966), Robert L. Holmes's *Nonviolence in Theory and Practice* (1990), and David P. Barash's *Approaches to Peace: A Reader in Peace Studies* (2000) all include William James's 1910 essay, "The Moral Equivalent of War," but nothing by Jane Addams.[97] One notable exception is the anthology edited by Staughton Lynd and Alice Lynd, *Nonviolence in America: A Documentary History* (1995), which includes both James's essay and a chapter from Addams's *Peace and Bread in Time of War.*[98]

A rare instance in which *Newer Ideals of Peace* has been anthologized is the inclusion of a brief excerpt from Addams's chapter on "The Passing of the War Virtues" in a collection edited by Arthur Weinberg and Lila Weinberg, *Instead of Violence: Writings by the Great Advocates of Peace and Nonviolence through History* (1963). It is perhaps indicative of a growing attention to Addams's ideas that this excerpt has been retained in a much shorter revised edition published by Beacon Press in 2002 under the title *The Power of Nonviolence: Writings by Advocates of Peace,* with an introduction by Howard Zinn and new selections ranging from Dorothy Day to Arundhati Roy.[99] Symbolically at least, this brings *Newer Ideals of Peace* into the circle of "writings of the great advocates of peace and nonviolence" who figure prominently today.

IX. A Legacy for Our Time

In his letter to Addams of February 1907, James had written: "Yours is a deeply original mind, and all so quiet and harmless! Yet revolutionary in the extreme." The revolutionary character of Addams's ideas, seemingly so "quiet and harmless," appears on careful reading of *Newer Ideals of Peace* in the broad sweep of her rejection, as inadequate or wrong, of a wide range of beliefs and practices of those concerned with war and peace in her time. Traditional peace advocates and internationalists, eighteenth-century philosophers and founders of the U.S. constitution, overt and covert militarists, and theories of democratic peace and liberal capitalism all fell under the scathing touch of her pen. But as Emma Goldman argued in her book on the Russian Revolution in 1922, the task of revolution is not primarily negative and destructive, it must be positive and constructive.[100] This was the task which Addams set herself in *Newer Ideals of Peace.*

In the sixth edition of *Peace and World Security Studies: A Curriculum Guide* (1994), J. Ann Tickner, writing on "Feminist Perspectives on Peace and World Security in the Post-Cold War Era," provides an unusual acknowledgment of the impact and relevance to the present of Jane Addams's ideas.[101] Tickner's comments on Addams, though brief, are insightful. Discussing how contemporary feminist theories and women in peace movements approach issues of international security, Tickner noted that "Jane Addams spoke of the need for a new internationalism to replace the self-destructive nationalism that contributed so centrally to the outbreak of [World War I]." The Nairobi Conference final document (1985), Tickner pointed out, argued that "security cannot be built on others' insecurity." In Tickner's view, the women at Nairobi, like Addams, offered multidimensional conceptions of security and peace "that included economic as well as military concerns" and were not zero-sum. "Jane Addams's views," she wrote, "dismissed at the time as impractical, are quite compatible with recent attempts to redefine security—efforts that have had an important influence on broadening the curriculum of peace and conflict studies."[102] This linking of Addams' ideas with contemporary redefinitions of international security important to peace and conflict studies today could be extended to many of the ideas put forward by Addams in *Newer Ideals of Peace* and in her later book, *Peace and Bread in Time of War* (1922), of which John Dewey had written that "the two books form a whole."[103]

Although as we have seen, *Newer Ideals of Peace* was not in fact dismissed "at the time" of its publication as impractical (on the contrary, praised by reviewers for its thorough grounding in reality and experience), it has sometimes been dismissed as such by those who have misread Addams as naïve. In fact, Addams was far from naïve about the real prospects for the kind of positive peace she sought. Rather, she was acutely aware of the formidable array of forces of militarism, exploitation, and oppression that would have to be overcome to achieve the "newer ideals of peace," and her analysis of these forces in the book constitutes a major part of her theoretical contribution.

The myth of Addams's naïveté in regard to war and peace has been pressed perhaps most strongly in Jean Elshtain's treatment of *Newer Ideals of Peace* in her 2002 biography, *Jane Addams and the Dream of American Democracy*. Though Elshtain sought to counter some distortions of Addams's ideas and respond to her detractors (see, for example, Elshtain, 19–28), she undermined this effort by her own distortions of Addams's words and by a rendering of Addams's vision that is at once dismissive and bordering on caricature, if not ridicule.

Thus Elshtain characterized Addams in this period as "expressing the standard progressive and evolutionary argument"[104] and sharing "the optimistic, sunny hopefulness of social evolutionists" (Elshtain, 202). She paraphrased Addams as follows:

Surely things could only get better, as her 1907 book *Newer Ideals of Peace* had *confidently predicted.* She was to be proven wrong [by World War I and after]. . . . The entry of women into political and social life would *surely* help push the war virtues aside and help nurture and sustain a group morality based on a solidarity that did not need external enemies in order to hold itself intact. . . . *Surely,* one day, the international arena in which states engage one another *would* find pacific modes of social exchange. The immigrant city had convinced Addams of this possibility (Elshtain, 202; emphasis added).

The italicized words in this paraphrased passage, however, were introduced by Elshtain, not by Addams, who never "confidently predicted" in *Newer Ideals of Peace* that "things could only get better" or that her vision "would" "surely" be reached.

On the contrary, Addams expressed again and again the tentative character and serious doubts of success of her vision, and never expected that it could have been achieved in the few years that elapsed between the writing of *Newer Ideals of Peace* and the outbreak of World War I. Certainly the war was a shock and severe disappointment to Addams, who recognized it as a terrible setback to the forces she had discerned as foundations for a future peace. But the image Elshtain portrays of Addams "shaking her head in puzzlement" at the malignant developments of the years following the publication of *Newer Ideals of Peace* fails abysmally to do justice to Addams even at the level of common sense, much less at the level of intellectual acuity.[105]

Throughout *Newer Ideals,* Addams's hopes for the future of those ideals were hedged with doubt and uncertainty:

One dares not grow too certain as to the wells of moral healing which lie under the surface of the sullen work-driven life which the industrial quarters of the modern city present. . . .(pp. 12–13); There *arises the hope* that when this newer patriotism becomes large enough, it will overcome arbitrary boundaries and soak up the notion of nationalism. We *may* then give up war. . . . These humble harbingers of the Newer Ideals of Peace, venturing themselves upon a larger relationship, are most touching; and while *the success of their efforts can never be guaranteed or spoken of too confidently,* they stir us with a strange hope . . . and *we almost come to believe* that such a foundation is, in fact, being laid now—not in speculation, but in action (pp. 13–14); In such undertakings [as the international campaign against tuberculosis and the social welfare policies and mutual benefit societies becoming prevalent in many countries] . . . are we beginning to see *the first timid forward reach* [of the international movements to abolish poverty and disease] (p. 17; for all italics, emphases added).

These remarks show that Addams was far from sure or confident of a "sunny" outcome for the newer ideals of peace. She perceived, if only in the shape of a "first timid forward reach," some hope for the achievement of her vision, but not at all in the short term, and only perhaps in the long term. Moreover, in a particularly important passage, Addams wrote:

It is possible that we shall be saved from warfare by the "fighting rabble" itself, by the "quarrelsome mob" turned into kindly citizens of the world through the pressure of a cosmopolitan neighborhood. *It is not that they are shouting for peace—on the contrary, if they shout at all, they will continue to shout for war*—but that they are really attaining cosmopolitan relations through daily experience. *They will probably believe for a long time that war is noble and necessary both to engender and cherish patriotism;* and yet all of the time, below their shouting, they are living in the kingdom of human kindness. . . . They are developing the only sort of patriotism consistent with the intermingling of the nations (p. 13, emphasis added).[106]

While this passage has been seen, correctly, as embodying a central argument of Addams's analysis of the role of ordinary people in the cosmopolitan neighborhood in bringing about the eventual attainment of peace, the reservations expressed alongside the cautious hopes have been given less attention. Far from taking a posture of naïve optimism, Addams stated clearly here that she expected the popular masses to "continue to shout for war" and to "believe for a long time that war is noble and necessary."

Elshtain unaccountably charges that Addams "omits from her analysis the pugnacity often visible in immigrant groups' dealings with one another; the alienation of the younger generation of immigrants from the elders, and the aura of fear and suspicion engendered by overbearing police raids and a hysterical press. These omissions permitted her to avoid the unhappy conclusion that there would *always* be forms of conflict, alienation, turmoil and suspicion between groups of people in cities as well as between states."[107]

Addams, however, did not omit those aspects of immigrant life—on the contrary, she elaborated on them at some length throughout the book. For example, the "alienation of the younger generation of immigrants from the elders" is specifically raised in her discussion of contemptuous attitudes towards and among immigrants: "This attitude of contempt," wrote Addams, "this survival of the spirit of the conqueror toward an inferior people, has many manifestations, but none so harmful as when it becomes absorbed and imitated and is finally evinced by the children of the foreigners toward their own parents" (p. 29). Addams went on to elaborate the point (pp. 29–30) in a passage so poignant that one wonders how Elshtain could possibly have forgotten it.

In a later passage summarizing Addams's views,[108] Elshtain, referring again to Addams's alleged "confident, prewar hope," concluded: "This is Jane Addams at her most optimistic and, arguably, her least persuasive. The horror of the slaughter on the Western front makes [Addams's] prewar optimism seem both naïve and forlorn. The idea of social evolution from militarism to nonmilitant internationalism is no longer convincing."[109]

This last point is indeed at the heart of Elshtain's dismissal of Addams's views. Elshtain, adopting what today is called a "realist" (i.e., conservative) stance in regard to international relations, rejects the notion that militarism can—or indeed, should—be overcome. She objects that Addams "describes the 'military party' or claim in wholly negative terms, as something that the human race can and should abandon altogether." She argues further that Addams "elides national defense and security with militarism and authoritarianism" and fails to consider "ways to provide for the common defense that do not incite contempt and cruelty." Instead, Elshtain concludes derisively, Addams "extols the blessings of a new dispensation: civic communion brought about through pacific means."[110]

Elshtain summons up against Addams the usual arguments of the conservative position, asserting the need for coercive authority and structure, the absence of these in the international arena, and "the pervasiveness of violence as a feature of all human cultures, past and present."[111] But she fails to come to grips with—or indeed to identify correctly—the essential core of Addams's "newer ideals of peace." Elshtain erroneously attributed to Addams the identification of her "newer ideals" with "the strengthening of international law" or "some form of international law or international organization that did not yet exist but that must be promoted and eventually secured."[112]

But as Sondra Herman made clear in *Eleven Against War,* Addams did not believe that international institutions or international law would bring true peace.[113] In *Newer Ideals of Peace,* Addams was respectful of such international bodies as the Interparliamentary Union for International Arbitration and the Institute of International Law, but she was skeptical that they went to the root of the problem of war or the foundation for peace (pp. 6–7).

Herman placed Addams in the context of a broad division of internationalist thought at the beginning of the twentieth century between adherents of an ideal of internationalist "polity" (coercive, institutional structures for resolution and control of conflicts at the interstate level) and adherents of an ideal of international "community," grounding peace in non-governmental associations and interactions among peoples across national and state boundaries, in economic, social, and cultural relations. Though the lines between the two schools of thought were not rigid or exclusive, and Herman found aspects of both positions in Jane Addams's ideas, she saw Addams as primarily in the camp of the communalists, along with such theorists as Josiah Royce and Thorstein Veblen.

Herman argued that where the advocates of international polity, such as Woodrow Wilson, Elihu Root, and Nicholas Murray Butler (with whom Addams shared the Nobel Peace Prize in 1931), accepted ideas of natural inequality and aggressiveness, adopting an individualist and atomistic conception of human relations in society, the communalists rejected Social Darwinism and held that as consciousness was formed in relationships, peace would evolve through an ever-changing dynamic process among diverse peoples. For Addams, what was necessary was to turn attention toward the mass of the people as the source and foundation for the evolution of peace.

Moreover, as Herman noted, the communalists rejected the equation of success with virtue or superiority, finding more promising virtues often among the "primitive" or conquered peoples.[114] Indeed, the word "primitive" to Addams was not a term of contempt, but of respect, as for the "simple people [who] regularly deplete their scanty livelihood in response to a primitive pity [and] . . . an unquenchable desire that charity and simple justice shall regulate men's relations" (p. 10). Or again: "after all, the things that make men alike are stronger and more primitive than the things that separate them" (p. 12).

Addams's vision was a communitarian one, in which the foundations of peace must lie in cooperation and social justice at all levels of society, local and global, political and economic. The long-term relevance of this approach to peace was reflected (though without specific reference to her) in the theme for the biennial conference of the International Peace Research Association in 1998: "Meeting Human Needs in a Cooperative World." What she offered, indeed, was the essential framework and core ideas of peace theory as it appears nearly a century later: the critique of militarized society and of social injustice, and a rejection of the "negative peace" of philosophers and pacifists of the past in favor of a concept of peace founded on social and economic justice, and grounded in communitarian (or today, "grass-roots") activism and networks—all aspects of what is generally termed "positive peace" in peace studies today.

Thus, for example, Addams would have found herself at home at the International Women's Working Conference on "Women and Children, Militarism, and Human Rights" held at Naha City, Okinawa, in May 1997, where forty women activists and researchers came together in an international network with a shared vision echoing much of what Addams had written ninety years earlier. As Gwyn Kirk and Margo Okazawa-Rey reported, "Our vision is for a sustainable, life-affirming future focusing on small-scale projects, local autonomy, and self-determination, with an emphasis on community land-use systems rather than private property. It includes the creation of true local democracies, the empowerment of local people, and the inclusion of women and children in decision-making. It will involve base conversion as well as nonmilitary approaches to resolving conflicts. It means promoting the value of socially responsible work, and the elimination of weapons-making industries."[115] The Okinawa workshop group also agreed "that we need a deeper understanding of demilitarization that goes beyond bases, land, and weapons, to include cultures, consciousness, and national identities." Echoing Addams's call for "the passing of the military virtues" and for "moral substitutes for war," the 1997 workshop participants argued further: "Given that masculinity in many countries, including the United States, is defined in military terms, [our vision] will also involve a redefinition of masculinity, strength, power, and adventure." And finally: "It will need appropriate learning and education, cultural activities, and values moving away from consumerism to sustainable living, where people can discover what it means to be more truly human."[116]

Was Addams indeed "proven wrong" by the history of warfare in the twentieth century, as Elshtain so confidently asserted? That it would be "a long time" before the "fighting rabble," the "quarrelsome mob," would stop shouting for war was clear to Addams in 1906, so it is no surprise that many are still shouting for war today. Yet in the early years of the twenty-first century we are witnessing a massive outpouring, on a worldwide scale, of nonviolent popular opposition to the "wars on terrorism" in Afghanistan, Iraq, and around the globe, as well as even more massive international movements against the resurgence today of rapacious global capitalism, militarism, and imperialism. As the *New York Times* suggested in an editorial on February 17, 2003, in response to the mobilization of ten million or more antiwar demonstrators around the world that weekend: "there may still be two superpowers on the planet: the United States and world public opinion."[117]

Indeed we may conclude that Addams's vision has advanced much beyond that "first timid forward reach" of the international movements to abolish war, poverty, and disease in her time. Whereas those who shared Addams's vision in 1906 were relatively few, Arundhati Roy could claim in a speech on "Confronting Empire" at the World Social Forum in 2003: "Remember this: We be many and they be few. They need us more than we need them."[118] Despite the persistence and destructive magnitude of violence, war, and poverty that the few can still impose today, the image with which Addams closed *Newer Ideals for Peace* in 1906 now represents the hopes and actions of growing millions around the world:

the prophet Isaiah . . . founded the cause of peace upon the cause of righteousness, not only as expressed in political relations, but also in industrial relations. He contended that peace could be secured only as men abstained from the gains of oppression and responded to the cause of the poor; that swords would finally be beaten into plowshares and pruning hooks, not because men resolved to be peaceful, but because all the metal of the earth would be turned to its proper use when the poor and their children should be abundantly fed. It was as if the ancient prophet foresaw that . . . peace would no longer be an absence of war, but the unfolding of world-wide processes making for the nurture of human life. (p. 131)

NOTES

1. See pp. x–xi above and n. 4 for discussion of the book's publication history. We are grateful to Chun-Hui Sophie Ho for research assistance in this project. For help in obtaining various documents and information, we thank: Suzanne Ward, Inter-Library Loan Office, Purdue University; Wendy E. Chmielewski, curator, Swarthmore College Peace Collection; Margaret Strobel, director, and Rima Lunin Schultz, assistant director, Jane Addams Hull-House Museum, University of Illinois at Chicago; and Margaret Kimball, university archivist of the Stanford University Libraries. We would also like to thank Joan Catapano, associate director and editor-in-chief of the University of Illinois Press, for her support and extraordinary patience with us in the lengthy process of preparing the introduction to this edition of *Newer Ideals of Peace*.

2. F. J. D. Scott, ed., *William James: Selected Unpublished Correspondence, 1885–1910* (Columbus: Ohio State University Press, 1986), 433. It does not appear, however, that James made public this remarkable assessment.

3. Jane Addams, second lecture on "The Newer Ideals of Peace," Wednesday, July 9, 1902, The *Chautauqua Assembly Herald 27*, 5 (July 10, 1902), 6. The first lecture was given two days earlier, on Monday, July 7, and appeared in *Chautauqua Assembly Herald 27*, 3 (July 8, 1902), 5.

4. Correspondence among Addams, Macmillan, and Ely concerning the development and publication of NIP extends from October 29, 1902 through December 17, 1906, and is available in the microfilm edition of *The Jane Addams Papers* (University Microfilms International, 1984), Reel 4. See also Allen F. Davis, *American Heroine: The Life and Legend of Jane Addams* (New York: Oxford University Press,

1973), 144–45. Davis's account, and most other references to *NIP*, give 1907 as its publication date, and most of the early copies we have seen specify a 1907 copyright and printing dates in January 1907 and later. Subsequent reprints by Macmillan in 1911 and 1915 give the 1907 copyright date. However, according to WorldCat, 21 copies with the 1906 copyright and December 1906 printing date are to be found in public and academic libraries in the U.S. today (January 2006).

5. Blanche Wiesen Cook, Charles Chatfield, and Sandi Cooper, eds., *The Garland Library of War and Peace: A Collection of 360 Titles Reprinted in 328 Volumes*, with an Introduction by Merle Curti (New York: Garland, 1971). This 136-page catalog lists the following works by Addams under the heading of "Peace Leaders: Biographies and Memoirs": Jane Addams, *Peace and Bread in Time of War* (1945, orig. 1922), reprinted together with her short address on "Patriotism and Pacifists in Wartime" (1917); and Jane Addams, Emily Greene Balch, and Alice Hamilton, *Women at The Hague: The International Congress of Women and Its Results* (1915). Under "Documentary Anthologies," the catalog also lists *Jane Addams on Peace and Freedom, 1914–1935,* a collection of essays and previously unpublished correspondence, edited by Blanche W. Cook. Not included in the catalog but published as part of the series in 1976 is a collection of speeches and short essays entitled *Jane Addams on Peace, War, and International Understanding, 1899–1932,* edited by Allen F. Davis.

6. The electronic version (showing the 1907 copyright date for the source) was entered on the internet during the years 1996–99 by the Mead Project at the Department of Sociology, Brock University, St. Catherines, Ontario, Canada (http://spartan.ac.brocku.ca/~lward/Addams_1907/Addams_1907_toc.htm). The 2004 paperback reprint was edited by Paul D. Sporer and published by Anza Classics Library at Chester, New York.

7. In the bibliography of Addams's writings appended to his *Beloved Lady: A History of Jane Addams' Ideas on Reform and Peace* (Baltimore, Md.: Johns Hopkins Press, 1967), John C. Farrell noted that Chapters II, III, and VII of *Newer Ideals of Peace* were revisions of previously published articles (respectively 1905, 1905, and 1906), and that chapters V and VIII contain material that first appeared in 1904, 1899, and 1905. For further details, see Farrell, 226.

8. James Weber Linn, *Jane Addams: A Biography* (New York: D. Appleton-Century, 1935), 292.

9. Addams's talk, given on Apr. 30, 1899, at the Chicago Liberty Meeting in the Central Music Hall, was printed as "Democracy or Militarism" in *Liberty Tract No. 1* (Chicago: Central Anti-Imperialist League, 1899), 35–39, and reprinted as "What Peace Means" in *Unity XLIII* (May 4, 1899), 178; later reprinted on the internet in Jim Zwick, ed., *Anti-Imperialism in the United States, 1898–1935,* at http://www.boondocksnet.com/ai/ (June 3, 2002).

Allen Davis remarks that Addams was "always a minor figure" in the anti-imperialist movement (Davis, *American Heroine*, n. 4 above, pp. 140–41). But Zwick notes that she served as a vice-president of the national Anti-Imperialist League

(1904–1919). She was also a co-founder of the American Union Against Militarism and a member of its Civil Liberties Bureau (later the American Civil Liberties Union) and the Woman's Peace Party (later Women's International League for Peace and Freedom), which took a strongly anti-imperialist stance in its critique of the Versailles Treaty in 1922. See Jane Addams, *Peace and Bread in Time of War* (New York: Women's International League for Peace and Freedom, U.S. Section, 1922, 1945. Reprinted by Garland, 1972, and University of Illinois Press, 2002).

10. This passage, somewhat reworked, reappears in the final paragraph of *NIP* in a concluding comment on the conception of peace envisioned by the Prophet Isaiah (p. 131).

11. [First lecture.] *Chautauqua Assembly Herald, July 8, 1902* (n. 3 above).

12. [Second lecture.] *Chautauqua Assembly Herald, July 10, 1902* (n. 3 above).

13. Ibid.

14. Ibid., 7.

15. Addams's handwritten diary entry for Sunday, May 3, 1903 reads: "11 A.M. Ethical Society. Moral Substitute for War." See *The Jane Addams Papers, 1860–1960* (Ann Arbor: University Microfilms International, 1984): *Reel 29, Frame 0903.* Advance notice of the talk appeared in the *Inter Ocean* (Chicago: Inter Ocean Publishers) on May 2, 1903, and excerpts from Addams's talk appeared under the title "End of All Wars in Sight" in the same periodical on May 4, 1903, p. 6 (clippings in *Jane Addams Papers, Reel 55, Frame 841*). Allen Davis, n. 4 above (*American Heroine*, 143) cited May 3, 1903, as the date of the *Inter Ocean* article, but that was the date of the talk itself. Four paragraphs of direct quotes from Addams appeared under the heading "A Moral Substitute for War" in *Friends Intelligencer 51* (Jan. 9, 1904), 30; this was most likely an excerpt from her May 1903 talk, and most of its content reappeared in *NIP.*

16. "Address [on] the Responsibilities and Duties of Women Toward the Peace Movement," in *Official Report of the Thirteenth Universal Peace Congress* (Boston: The Peace Congress Committee, 1904), 120–23; "Address [on] the Interests of Labor in International Peace," ibid., 145–47; "Address [at] Peace Congress Banquet," ibid., 261–62.

17. Quincy Wright, *A Study of War* (Chicago: University of Chicago Press, 1942, reprinted 1965), 1089–93, 1098, 1305–7. Martin Luther King, Jr., *Stride Toward Freedom* (New York: Harper, 1958), 31–32, and *Why We Can't Wait* (New York: New American Library, 1964), 84–85. While their definitions of negative and positive peace differ, both authors show a strong preference for positive peace as a social and political goal.

18. See also Mary Wollstonecraft, *A Vindication of the Rights of Men* (1790): "Security of property! Behold, in a few words, the definition of English liberty. . . . But softly—it is only the property of the rich that is secure; the man who lives by the sweat of his brow has no asylum from oppression." In Hilda L. Smith and Berenice A. Carroll, eds., *Women's Political and Social Thought: An Anthology* (Bloomington: Indiana University Press, 2000), 159.

19. On Josiah Royce and the relationship of his ideas to those of Addams, see Sondra R. Herman, *Eleven Against War: Studies in American Internationalist Thought, 1898–1921* (Stanford, Calif.: Hoover Institution Press, Stanford University, 1969), chapter IV: 86–113.

20. A. Roserot, ed., *Mme de Chastenay, Mémoires, 1717–1815,* vol. 2, 2nd ed. (Paris: E Plon, 1897), 201. Cited by Volker R. Berghahn, *Militarism: The History of an International Debate, 1861–1979* (Leamington Spa, Warwickshire: Berg Publishers, 1981), 7. The passage can also be found in the one-volume edition by Guy Chaussinand-Nogaret (Paris: Librairie Académique Perrin, 1987), 470 (translation by B. A. Carroll). The way the term is used here, however, suggests that it may have been in more general usage when de Chastenay wrote these words. The word "militarist" itself was used two centuries earlier by William Shakespeare to mean simply a soldier. On Louise-Marie-Victorine, Comtesse de Chastenay-Lanty (1771–1835), author of historical and literary works, see Elizabeth D. Schafer, biographical sketch in D. R. Woolf, ed., *A Global Encyclopedia of Historical Writing,* vol. 1 (New York: Garland Publishing, 1998), 154. See also Marilyn Yalom, *Blood Sisters: The French Revolution in Women's Memory* (New York: Basic Books, 1993).

21. Berghahn, *Militarism* (n. 19 above), 9.

22. Ibid., 11; Herbert Spencer, *The Principles of Sociology,* vol. II/2 (New York, 1886), 568–642.

23. Sondra Herman, "Jane Addams: The Community as a Neighborhood," in her *Eleven Against War* (n. 19 above), 114–49. On Spencer, see especially 9, 129, 132–33. For a different viewpoint, note Marilyn Fischer, "Herbert Spencer and Addams' Newer Ideals of Peace: or How Addams Transmuted Spencer's Racist, Sexist 19th Century Evolutionary Theory into a Liberatory Pacifism," paper delivered at the North American Society for Social Philosophy, Eastern Michigan University, Ypsilanti, Mich., July 26–28, 2001; see also Fischer's introduction to the 2003 Thoemmes Press reprint edition of *NIP* (see n. 95 below).

24. Addams, "Democracy or Militarism," in Zwick, *Anti-Imperialism,* 2.

25. Ibid.

26. Rosa Luxemburg, "Rede über den Völkerfrieden, den Militarismus und die stehenden Heere" [Sept. 27, 1900], in *Gesammelte Werke,* Institut für Marxismus-Leninismus beim ZK der SED, vol. 1 (Berlin: Dietz Verlag, 1974), 807–9 (translations from the German text by B. A. Carroll). See also Anneliese Laschitza, *Im Lebensrausch, trotz alledem Rosa Luxemburg: eine Biographie* (Berlin: Aufbau-Verlag, 1996), 156–58. We are indebted to Kevin Anderson for assistance in locating these sources.

27. Luxemburg, "Rede über den Völkerfrieden." See also the recent reprint edition of Rosa Luxemburg, *The Accumulation of Capital* [1913] (New York: Routledge, 2003).

28. Karl Liebknecht, *Militarism and Anti-Militarism* [1907], trans. Alexander Sirnis; introduction by Philip S. Foner (New York: Dover, 1972), 39 [original italics].

See also Karl Liebknecht, "The Necessity of Proletarian Young People's Organizations," Congress of the Social-Democratic Party at Barmen, 1904, in *Speeches of Karl Liebknecht* (New York: International Publishers, 1927), 26–28.

29. The resolutions against militarism of the international congresses at Paris in 1889, Brussels in 1891, and London in 1896, to which Luxemburg referred in 1900, may well have been known to Addams, who, as noted above, referred specifically to the congresses of 1864 and 1868 in her 1899 speech on "Democracy and Militarism" (see n. 9 above).

30. William James, *The Varieties of Religious Experience* (New York: Longmans, Green, 1902; reprinted, Modern Library, 1929), 359.

31. Addams, "Democracy or Militarism" (n. 9 above), in Zwick, *Anti-Imperialism*, 3.

32. Jane Addams, "Address [at] Peace Congress Banquet" (n. 16 above), 261–62.

33. An earlier reference to the idea of finding a substitute for war had been made by W. Randal Cremer, who founded the Workman's Peace Association about the year 1872, described as the "first attempt to establish a specifically working-class peace society in England." See Sandi E. Cooper, *Patriotic Pacifism: Waging War on War in Europe, 1815–1914* (New York: Oxford University Press, 1991), 48. Cooper notes that "Cremer asserted that 'sooner or later, a substitute must and will be found for war,' and declared that workers will play their part in moving that day along." See also Howard Evans, *Sir Randal Cremer* (London, 1909; reprinted in the Garland Library of War and Peace, 1973).

34. Jane Addams, "The Interests of Labor in International Peace" (n. 16 above), 145–46.

35. "Address [at] Peace Congress Banquet" (n. 16 above), 261.

36. Ibid.

37. William James, "Address [at] Peace Congress Banquet," in Official Report of the Thirteenth Universal Peace Congress (Boston: The Peace Congress Committee, 1904), 266–69.

38. Ibid., 267.

39. Ibid., 268.

40. Scott (ed.), *James Correspondence* (n. 2 above), 433.

41. William James, "The Moral Equivalent of War," *International Conciliation*, No. 27 (Feb. 1910). Reprinted in Staughton Lynd and Alice Lynd (eds.), *Nonviolence in America: A Documentary History,* revised edition (Maryknoll, N.Y.: Orbis Books, 1995), 65–75 [page 73, emphasis added]. This essay has been reprinted many times.

42. James, "Moral Equivalent of War," 147–48.

43. Hilda L. Smith, *All Men and Both Sexes: Gender, Politics, and the False Universal in England, 1640–1832* (University Park: Pennsylvania State University Press, 2002).

44. Linda Schott, "Jane Addams and William James on Alternatives to War," *Journal of the History of Ideas* 54 (1993), 253.

45. One early review of *NIP* ("How to supplant the military ideal," *Current Lit-*

erature XLII, Apr. 1907, p. 417) began by characterizing the book as Addams's effort to solve the problem posed by William James, of discovering a "moral equivalent of war." In *American Heroine* (n. 4 above), Allen Davis titled his chapter on Addams's peace work before 1914 "A moral equivalent of war."

46. Sondra Herman notes, in relation to Addams's confidence in the underlying kindness and the self-governing creative promise of human beings, her interest in "the play instinct" and children's imagination, citing *NIP* 171–72 (p. 95) and other writings (*Eleven Against War,* n. 23 above, 130). For a view of some more recent related ideas on nurturing "the least germ of promise," see the discussion of a "democratic conception of newness" in Berenice A. Carroll, "The Politics of 'Originality': Women and the class system of the intellect," *Journal of Women's History* 2, 2 (Fall 1990), 136–61, especially 153–59.

47. Jane Addams (ed.), *Hull-House Maps and Papers, a presentation of nationalities and wages in a congested district of Chicago, together with comments and essays on problems growing out of the social conditions, by residents of Hull-House, a social settlement at 235 South Halsted Street, Chicago, Ill.* (New York: T. Y. Crowell [Library of Economics and Politics, No. 5], 1895; reprinted New York: Arno Press, 1970).

48. See further Addams's discussion of the organization of the Russian *mir* in NIP (p. 39).

49. W.I. Thomas, in his "Votes for Women," *American Magazine* 68 (1909), 292–301 (http://spartan.ac.brocku.ca/lward/thomas/Thomas_1909_b.html), cited an argument of suffragists that "the 'ancient kindliness which sat beside the cradle of the race' has been put out of business by business, and that its restoration is even now being advocated more by women than by men" (294). The phrase seems therefore to have been in common usage in the suffrage movement by 1909, but we have not been able to identify its source. Thomas's argument in this article is marred by some of the worst appeals to racism and classism used by some of the suffragists at that time.

50. Jane Addams, "The Progressive Party and the Negro," *Crisis* 5 (Nov. 1912), 30.

51. Langston Hughes, *Fight for Freedom, the Story of the NAACP* (New York: W. W. Norton, 1962), excerpt reprinted in Joanne Grant, ed., *Black Protest: History, Documents, and Analyses, 1619 to the Present* (Greenwich, Conn.: Fawcett Publications, 1968), 211; Davis, *American Heroine* (n. 4, above), 129.

52. Ida B. Wells-Barnett, *Crusade for Justice: The Autobiography of Ida B. Wells,* ed. Alfreda M. Duster (Chicago: University of Chicago Press, 1970), 259–60, 276–78, 321–22. See also Bettina Aptheker, ed., *Lynching and Rape: An Exchange of Views* (New York: American Institute for Marxist Studies, 1977), Introduction: 6–7.

53. Wells-Barnett, *Crusade for Justice,* 259–60; Aptheker, *Lynching and Rape,* 6.

54. Jane Addams, "Respect for Law," *Independent* (Jan. 3, 1901), 18–20; also reprinted in Aptheker, *Lynching and Rape,* 22–27.

55. Aptheker, *Lynching and Rape,* 7; see also Wells-Barnett, *Crusade for Justice,* 321–22.

56. Jane Addams, "The Progressive Party and the Negro" (n. 50 above).

57. "Jane Addams Condemns Race Prejudice Film: Calls It 'Pernicious Carica-ture of Negro Race,'" *New York Evening Post*, Mar. 13, 1915.

58. See Mary Church Terrell, *A Colored Woman in a White World* (Washington, D.C.: National Association of Colored Women's Clubs, 1940), 328–35; also Carrie A. Foster, *The Women and the Warriors: The U.S. Section of the Women's International League for Peace and Freedom, 1915–1946* (Syracuse, N.Y.: Syracuse University Press, 1995), 157–60. The resolution on "Race Equality" was published among the appendices to the 1945 edition of Jane Addams, *Peace and Bread in Time of War*, and reprinted in the 1972 edition published in *The Garland Library of War and Peace* (New York: Garland Publishing, 1972), 263. This resolution was an extraordinary event in the history of the peace movement in 1919, but is unfortunately omitted, along with most of the resolutions of the congress, from the appendices to the 2002 reprint edition of *Peace and Bread* by the University of Illinois Press. See also Foster on the 1921 controversy between Terrell and the board of the Women's International League for Peace and Freedom (WILPF) concerning allegations of sexual assault by black occupation troops on German women, and Addams's support for Terrell's views on this matter (Foster, 159–60). See also Joyce Blackwell, *No Peace Without Freedom: Race and the Women's International League for Peace and Freedom, 1915–1975* (Carbondale: Southern Illinois University Press, 2004), 37–41, 43, 68, 95–96, 145.

59. Wells-Barnett's important earlier writings on lynching included *Southern Horrors: Lynch Law in All Its Phases* (1892); *A Red Record: Tabulated Statistics and Alleged Causes of Lynchings in the United States, 1892–1893–1894* (1895); and *Mob Rule in New Orleans* (1900), all first published by the author. For a recent edition, see Jacqueline Jones Royster, ed., *Southern Horrors and Other Writings: The Anti-Lynching Campaign of Ida B. Wells, 1892–1900* (Boston: St. Martin's Press, 1997). See also the extensive treatment of Wells's anti-lynching campaign by Patricia A. Schechter in *Ida B. Wells-Barnett and American Reform, 1880–1930* (Chapel Hill: University of North Carolina Press, 2001), 75–168.

60. Aptheker (n. 52 above), 8–14. Wells-Barnett's reply to Addams, entitled "Lynching and the Excuse for It," appeared in *Independent* on May 16, 1901; reprinted in Aptheker, 28–34. Aptheker also noted examples of Addams's problematic comments on black women in other works, including *Democracy and Social Ethics* and *A New Conscience and an Ancient Evil* (Aptheker, 35–36, n.9).

61. Aptheker, *Lynching and Rape* (n. 52 above), 17.

62. Schechter, *Ida B. Wells* (n. 59 above), 125.

63. Jane Addams, "The Progressive Party and the Negro" (n. 50 above), 31.

64. Linn, *Jane Addams* (n. 8 above), 294.

65. *American Monthly Review of Reviews* 35, 3 (Mar. 1907), 381.

66. *Annals of the American Academy of Political and Social Science* 29, 2 (Mar. 1907), 409.

67. George Herbert Mead, review of *NIP*, *American Journal of Sociology* 13, 1 (July 1907), 128.

68. Olivia Howard Dunbar, "Newer Ideals of Peace," *North American Review* DCXII (Apr. 5, 1907), 763.

69. *Literary Digest* 34, 11 (16 Mar. 1907), 433.

70. Linn, *Jane Addams* (n. 8 above), 294. See also Roosevelt's irate comments in "Tolstoy," published in the *Outlook*, May 15, 1909, 103–5; reprinted in the Thoemmes Press 2003 edition of *NIP* (see n. 95 below), 173–76. Without naming Addams, Roosevelt derided her "book on municipal problems, which ascribed our ethical and social shortcomings in municipal matters in part to the sin of 'militarism,'" asserting that in America, militarism "has not the smallest effect one way or the other; it is a negligible quantity."

71. Cited by Davis, *American Heroine* (n. 4 above), 148.

72. *Advocate of Peace* 69, 3 (Mar. 1907), 68–69.

73. *Nation* 84, (7 Mar. 1907), 247–48.

74. Nevertheless, according to royalty statements from Macmillan, they continued to sell a few copies of *NIP* annually until 1931. See the microfilmed *Jane Addams Papers* (n. 15 above), Reel 30, Frame 1717.

75. For evidence of the ongoing influence of the ideas Addams had put forward in *NIP,* see for example Carrie A. Foster, *The Women and the Warriors* (n. 58 above). See also Harriet Hyman Alonso, *Peace as a Women's Issue: A History of the U.S. Movement for World Peace and Women's Rights* (Syracuse, N.Y.: Syracuse University Press, 1993).

76. John Dewey, "Democratic Versus Coercive International Organization: The Realism of Jane Addams" (orig. 1945) in Jane Addams, *Peace and Bread in Time of War* and *Patriotism and Pacifists in War Time,* with a new introduction for the Garland Edition by Blanche Wiesen Cook (New York: Garland Publishing, 1972), xii–xiii.

77. Several paragraphs in the following pages are revised and condensed from Carroll, "The Politics of 'Originality'" (n. 46 above), 140–41.

78. Merle Curti, "Jane Addams on Human Nature," *Journal of the History of Ideas* 22, 2 (1961), 240–41.

79. Ibid. Sad to report, Curti also omitted any mention of Jane Addams and her ideas on human nature from his later book on this subject, *Human Nature in American Thought: A History* (Madison: University of Wisconsin Press, 1980).

80. Leonard Levy, Foreword, in Christopher Lasch, ed., *The Social Thought of Jane Addams* (Indianapolis: Bobbs Merrill, 1965), vii.

81. Christopher Lasch, Introduction, in Lasch, *The Social Thought of Jane Addams* (n. 80 above), xv.

82. See Linda Gordon, Persis Hunt, Elizabeth Pleck, Rochelle Goldberg Ruthchild, and Marcia Scott, "Historical Phallacies: Sexism in American Historical Writing," in Berenice A. Carroll, ed., *Liberating Women's History: Theoretical and Critical Essays* (Urbana: University of Illinois Press, 1976), 61–62.

83. Farrell completed his book in 1965, before the appearance of Lasch's anthology, but it was published posthumously two years later. For Farrell's account of the development of Addams's ideas about moral substitutes for war and of the main points that she made in *Newer Ideals of Peace,* see *Beloved Lady* (n. 7 above), 143–47.

84. Herman, *Eleven Against War* (n. 19 and 23 above).

85. In Edward T. James, Janet Wilson James, and Paul S. Boyer, eds., *Notable American Women: A Biographical Dictionary* (Cambridge, Mass.: Belknap/Harvard University Press, 1971), 1: 21. This remark is especially strange in view of the fact that Scott had provided an illuminating introduction to the Belknap Press reprint edition of *Democracy and Social Ethics* in 1964. See Ann Firor Scott, Introduction, in Jane Addams, *Democracy and Social Ethics* (Cambridge, Mass.: Belknap/Harvard University Press, 1964).

86. Davis, *American Heroine* (n. 4 above), xi. Davis's new introduction for the 2000 reprint edition of his book makes no change in this assessment.

87. Daniel Levine, *Jane Addams and the Liberal Tradition* (Madison: State Historical Society of Wisconsin, 1972), xviii.

88. Ibid., x.

89. Many scholars of intellectual history, including Arthur O. Lovejoy, Robert K. Merton, Roger Shattuck, and Pitirim O. Sorokin, have questioned the notion of "originality" and demonstrated that in the history of ideas, there are always predecessors, and predecessors to the predecessors. As Morroe Berger put it, "Ideas may be traced back infinitely because they emerge out of previous ones and out of a social condition that has its origins in previous ones too." See further Carroll, "The Politics of 'Originality'" (n. 46 above), 141–47.

90. Mary Jo Deegan, *Jane Addams and the Men of the Chicago School, 1892–1918* (New Brunswick, N.J.: Transaction Books, 1988). The passing suggestion that "an image of womanhood" would be "stigmatizing" in assessing a person's intellectual work is telling. Deegan argues that "Addams profoundly affected the course of American sociology. . . . She is the key to understanding an era and a discipline" (Deegan, 14–15). Deegan shows how the work of Addams and other women at Hull-House as well as the "extensive network of women sociologists" with whom she worked was selectively appropriated without acknowledgment by the renowned male sociologists of the Chicago School. "This book documents the process of selectively using Addams's social thought in sociology while denying her . . . sociological leadership" (Deegan, 14).

91. Lynn McDonald, *The Women Founders of the Social Sciences* (Ottawa: Carleton University Press, 1994). Patricia Madoo Lengermann and Jill Niebrugge-Brantley, eds., *The Women Founders: Sociology and Social Theory, 1830–1930—A Text/Reader* (Boston: McGraw-Hill, 1998).

92. Charlene Seigfried, *Pragmatism and Feminism: Reweaving the Social Fabric* (Chicago: University of Chicago Press, 1996); Introduction to the Illinois Edition, in Jane Addams, *Democracy and Social Ethics* (Urbana: University of Illinois Press, 2002); and Introduction to the Illinois Edition, in Jane Addams, *The Long Road of Woman's Memory* (Urbana: University of Illinois Press, 2002).

93. Jean Bethke Elshtain, *Jane Addams and the Dream of American Democracy: A Life* (New York: Basic Books, 2002) and Elshtain, ed., *The Jane Addams Reader* (New York: Basic Books, 2002).

94. Schott, "Jane Addams and William James" (n. 44 above).

95. In 2003, a four-volume set of Addams's writings on peace was published in hardcover by Thoemmes Press (London) in its series on the History of American Thought. The collection is co-edited by Marilyn Fischer and Judy D. Whipps. It comprises reprint editions of *Newer Ideals of Peace, Women at The Hague,* and *Peace and Bread in Time of War,* together with reviews and letters, plus a volume of selected shorter writings on peace (articles and speeches). Volume 1 contains *Newer Ideals of Peace* with seventeen reviews and an introduction by Marilyn Fischer. Fischer and Whipps have contributed thoughtful introductions to these volumes.

96. See for example: Kathryn Kish Sklar, "Jane Addams's Peace Activism, 1914–1922: A Model for Women Today?" *Women's Studies Quarterly* 23, 3 & 4 (Fall/Winter 1995), 32–47; Harriet Hyman Alonso, "Nobel Peace Laureates, Jane Addams and Emily Greene Balch: Two Women of WILPF," *Journal of Women's History* 7, 2 (Summer 1995), 6–26; see also the exchange between Mary Jo Deegan and Alonso in the summer 1996 issue (8, 2), 121–29. Both Sklar and Alonso give attention to Addams's ideas, but focus mainly on issues of activism.

97. Peter Mayer, ed., *The Pacifist Conscience* (Chicago: Henry Regnery, 1967); Robert L. Holmes, ed., *Nonviolence in Theory and Practice* (Belmont, Calif.:Wadsworth, 1990); David P. Barash, *Approaches to Peace: A Reader in Peace Studies* (New York: Oxford University Press, 2000).

98. Jane Addams, "Personal Reactions During War," chapter 7 of *Peace and Bread in Time of War* (see n. 9 above), in Staughton Lynd and Alice Lynd, eds., *Nonviolence in America* (1995) (n. 41 above). Staughton Lynd had included the same chapter by Addams in the first edition of this collection (Bobbs-Merrill, 1966).

99. Jane Addams, excerpt from *Newer Ideals of Peace,* in *The Power of Nonviolence: Writings by Advocates of Peace.* A Beacon Anthology (Boston: Beacon Press, 2002), 39–41. The same excerpt appeared in an earlier version of the anthology *Instead of Violence,* ed. Arthur Weinberg and Lila Weinberg (New York: Grossman Publishers, 1963), 305–7.

100. Emma Goldman, *My Disillusionment in Russia* (New York: Thomas Y. Crowell (Apollo), 1970 [1923, 1925]), 244. For discussion of Goldman's ideas on the "reconstructive" and "constructive" dimensions of revolution, see Berenice A. Carroll, "Emma Goldman and the Theory of Revolution," to appear in Penny Weiss and Loretta Kensinger, eds., *Feminist Interpretations of Emma Goldman,* forthcoming (University Park: Pennsylvania State University Press).

101. J. Ann Tickner, "Feminist Perspectives on Peace and World Security in the Post-Cold War Era," in Michael T. Klare, ed., *Peace and World Security Studies* [previously *Peace and World Order Studies*]: *A Curriculum Guide*—Sixth Edition (Boulder/London: Lynne Reinner, 1994), 43–54. It may be noted, however, that this is the only article in the volume that mentions Jane Addams, in a collection of more than 400 pages of articles and syllabi in peace studies.

102. Ibid., 44, 45.

103. Dewey, "Democratic Versus Coercive International Organization" (n. 76 above), xii.

104. Intentionally or not, this phrase implies that Addams's "newer ideals" in *NIP* were not at all new, but rather, unoriginal and derivative expressions of a "standard" argument.

105. Elshtain, *Jane Addams and the Dream* (n. 93 above), 203.

106. See Rosa Luxemburg's defense before the judges at her trial for anti-militarism in 1914, in Peter Nettl, *Rosa Luxemburg* (London: Oxford University Press, 2 vols., 1966) 2:488–92.

107. Elshtain, *Jane Addams and the Dream* (n. 93 above), 202 [italics by Elshtain].

108. Elshtain gives the following paraphrase: "The 'progressive goodness of the race' was close at hand," *Jane Addams and the Dream* (n. 93 above), 218. But while Addams did express belief in the "progressive goodness" of the human race, nowhere did she suggest that its realization in perfect peace or the end of conflict was "close at hand."

109. Ibid.

110. Ibid., 218–19.

111. Ibid., 219–21.

112. Ibid., 217, 220–21.

113. See Herman's introductory chapter, "Polity and Community: Two Ideals of International Society," *Eleven Against War* (n. 19 above), 1–21, especially 6–10, 20–21.

114. Ibid., 15.

115. Gwyn Kirk and Margo Okazawa-Rey, "Making Connections: Building an East Asia–U.S. Women's Network against U.S. Militarism," in Lois Ann Lorentzen and Jennifer Turpin, eds., *The Women and War Reader* (New York: New York University Press, 1998), 119.

116. Ibid. Another example of the reprise of one of Addams's ideas in recent years is Jonathan M. Hansen's *The Lost Promise of Patriotism: Debating American Identity, 1890–1920* (Chicago: University of Chicago Press, 2003). Without commenting on Addams's use of the term "cosmic patriotism" (see *NIP* p. 131), Hansen provides a useful exposition of what he calls "cosmopolitan patriotism" in her writings from an article of 1898 to *NIP* in 1906.

117. Patrick E. Tyler, "A New Power in the Streets," *New York Times*, Feb. 17, 2003. Reprinted online by the Freedom of Information Center, Feb. 18, 2003. See also "Grassroots Globalization Gets Real," by Kevin Danaher and Jason Mark, n.d. [Feb. 2003], http://globalenvision.org/library/8/392; and "A Rising New Force in World Public Opinion" by Immanuel Wallerstein, www.globalenvision.org/library/8/580; reprinted with permission from YaleGlobal Online, Jan. 28, 2004. Wallerstein reported on the 2004 meeting of the World Global Forum at Mumbai, India, which reflected the rapid growth of a worldwide movement dedicated to the vision that "another world is possible."

118. Arundhati Roy, *War Talk* (Cambridge, Mass.: South End Press, 2003), 112.

Appendix

CROSS-REFERENCE PAGINATION KEY
TO 1906 (1907) EDITION

✍ The table below provides a pagination key from this Illinois edition of *Newer Ideals of Peace* to the original Macmillan edition, for citations to the Addams text in this introduction. The cross-reference page numbers in the 1906 (1907) edition are shown in boldface.

Newer Ideals
of Peace

Prefatory Note

These studies in the gradual development of the moral substitutes for war have been made in the industrial quarter of a cosmopolitan city where the morality exhibits marked social and international aspects.

Parts of two chapters have been published before in the form of addresses, and two others as articles in the *North American Review* and in the *American Journal of Sociology.* All of them however are held together by a conviction that has been maturing through many years.

Hull-House, Chicago

I

Introduction

☙ The following pages present the claims of the newer, more aggressive ideals of peace, as over against the older dove-like ideal. These newer ideals are active and dynamic, and it is believed that if their forces were made really operative upon society, they would, in the end, quite as a natural process, do away with war. The older ideals have required fostering and recruiting, and have been held and promulgated on the basis of a creed. Their propaganda has been carried forward during the last century in nearly all civilized countries by a small body of men who have never ceased to cry out against war and its iniquities and who have preached the doctrines of peace along two great lines. The first has been the appeal to the higher imaginative pity, as it is found in the modern, moralized man. This line has been most effectively followed by two Russians, Count Tolstoy in his earlier writings and Verestchagin in his paintings. With his relentless power of reducing all life to personal experience Count Tolstoy drags us through the campaign of the common soldier in its sordidness and meanness and constant sense of perplexity. We see nothing of the glories we have associated with warfare, but learn of it as it appears to the untutored peasant who goes forth at the mandate of his superior to suffer hunger, cold, and death for issues which he does not understand, which, indeed, can have no moral significance to him. Verestchagin covers his canvas with thousands of wretched wounded and neglected dead, with the waste, cruelty, and squalor of war, until he forces us to question whether a moral issue can ever be subserved by such brutal methods.

High and searching as is the preaching of these two great Russians who hold their art of no account save as it serves moral ends, it is still the appeal of dogma, and may be reduced to a command to cease from evil. And when this same line of appeal is presented by less gifted men, it often results in mere sentimentality, totally unenforced by a call to righteousness.

The second line followed by the advocates of peace in all countries has been the appeal to the sense of prudence, and this again has found its ablest exponent in a Russian subject, the economist and banker, Jean de Bloch. He sets forth the cost of warfare with pitiless accuracy, and demonstrates that even the present armed peace is so costly that the burdens of it threaten social revolution in almost every country in Europe. Long before the reader comes to the end of de Bloch's elaborate computation he is ready to cry out on the inanity of the proposition that the only way to secure eternal peace is to waste so much valuable energy and treasure in preparing for war that war becomes impossible. Certainly no theory could be devised which is more cumbersome, more roundabout, more extravagant, than the *reductio ad absurdum* of the peace-secured-by-the-preparation-for-war theory. This appeal to prudence was constantly emphasized at the first Hague Conference and was shortly afterward demonstrated by Great Britain when she went to war in South Africa, where she was fined one hundred million pounds and lost ten thousand lives. The fact that Russia also, and the very Czar who invited the Conference disregarded the conclusions of the Hague Tribunal makes this line of appeal at least for the moment seem impotent to influence empires which command enormous resources and which lodge the power of expenditure in officials who have nothing to do with accumulating the treasure they vote to expend.

It would, however, be the height of folly for responsible statesmen to ignore the sane methods of international discussion and concession which have been evolved largely as a result of these appeals. The Interparliamentary Union for International Arbitration and the Institute of International Law represent the untiring efforts of the advocates of peace through many years. Nevertheless universal peace, viewed from the point of the World's Sovereignty or of the Counsel of Nations, is discouraging even when stated by the most ardent promoters of the peace society. Here it is quite possible that the mistake is being repeated which the old annalists of history made when they never failed to chronicle the wars and calamities which harassed their contemporaries, although, while the few indulged in fighting, the mass of them peacefully prosecuted their daily toil and followed their own conceptions of kindliness and equity. An English writer[1] has recently bidden us to look at the actual state of affairs existing at the present moment. He says, "Universal and permanent peace may be a vision; but the gradual change whereby war, as a normal state of international relations, has given place to peace as the normal state, is no vision, but an actual process of history palpably forwarded in our own day by the development of international law and of morals, and voluntary arbitration based thereon." He insists that it is the function of international lawyers merely to give coherent expression to the best principles which the common moral sense of civilized Governments recognizes; in other words, that international law should be like primitive law within the nation, a formal expression of custom resting on the sense of a reciprocal restraint which has been found to be necessary for the common good.

Assuming that the two lines of appeal—the one to sensibility and the other to prudence—will persist, and that the international lawyers, in spite of the fact that they have no court before which to plead and no executive to enforce their findings, will continue to formulate into codes the growing moral sense of the nations, the following pages hope not only to make clear the contention that these forces within society are so dynamic and vigorous that the impulses to war seem by comparison cumbersome and mechanical, but also to point out the development of those newer social forces which it is believed will at last prove a "sovereign intervention" by extinguishing the possibility of battle at its very source.

It is difficult to formulate the newer dynamic peace, embodying the later humanism, as over against the old dogmatic peace. The word "non-resistance" is misleading, because it is much too feeble and inadequate. It suggests passivity, the goody-goody attitude of ineffectiveness. The words "overcoming," "substituting," "re-creating," "readjusting moral values," "forming new centres of spiritual energy" carry much

1. L. T. Hobhouse, *Democracy and Reaction,* page 197.

more of the meaning implied. For it is not merely the desire for a conscience at rest, for a sense of justice no longer outraged, that would pull us into new paths where there would be no more war nor preparations for war. There are still more strenuous forces at work reaching down to impulses and experiences as primitive and profound as are those of struggle itself. That "ancient kindliness which sat beside the cradle of the race," and which is ever ready to assert itself against ambition and greed and the desire for achievement, is manifesting itself now with unusual force, and for the first time presents international aspects.

Moralists agree that it is not so much by the teaching of moral theorems that virtue is to be promoted as by the direct expression of social sentiments and by the cultivation of practical habits; that in the progress of society sentiments and opinions have come first, then habits of action and lastly moral codes and institutions. Little is gained by creating the latter prematurely, but much may be accomplished to the utilization of human interests and affections. The Advocates of Peace would find the appeal both to Pity and Prudence totally unnecessary, could they utilize the cosmopolitan interest in human affairs with the resultant social sympathy that at the present moment is developing among all the nations of the earth.

By way of illustration, I may be permitted to cite the London showman who used to exhibit two skulls of Shakespeare—one when he was a youth and went poaching, another when he was a man and wrote plays. There was such a striking difference between the roystering boy indulging in illicit sport and the mature man who peopled the London stage with all the world, that the showman grew confused and considered two separate acts of creation less improbable than that such an amazing change should have taken place. We can easily imagine the gifted youth in the little group of rustics at Stratford-on-Avon finding no adequate outlet for his powers save in a series of break-neck adventures. His only alternative was to sit by the fire with the village cronies, drinking ale so long as his shillings held out. But if we follow him up to London, through all the charm and wonder of the stage which represented his unfolding mind, if we can imagine his delight as he gradually gained the freedom, not only of that big town, but of the human city as well, we can easily see that illicit sport could no longer attract him. To have told the great dramatist the night Hamlet first stepped upon the boards that it was a wicked thing to poach, to have cautioned him that he must consider the cost of preserving the forest and of raising the deer, or to have made an appeal to his pity on behalf of the wounded creatures, would have been the height of folly, because totally unnecessary. All desire, almost all memory of those days, had dropped from him, through his absorption in the great and exciting drama of life. His effort to understand it, to portray it, had utilized and drained his every power. It is equally true of our contemporaries, as it was of the great playwright, that the attainment of this all-absorbing passion for multiform life, with the desire to understand its mysteries and to free its capacities, is gradually displacing the juvenile propensities to warfare. From this standpoint the advocates of the newer Ideals of Peace would have little to do but to insist that the social point of view be kept paramount, realizing at the same time that the social sentiments are as blind as the egoistic sentiments and must be enlightened, disciplined and directed by the fullest knowledge. The modern students of human morality have told us that primitive man, by the very necessities of his hard struggle for life, came at last to identify his own existence with that of his tribe.

Tribal life then made room within itself for the development of that compassion which is the first step towards sensibility and higher moral sentiment. If we accept this statement then we must assume that the new social morality, which we so sadly need, will of necessity have its origin in the social affections—we must search in the dim borderland between compassion and morality for the beginnings of that cosmopolitan affection, as it is prematurely called.

The life of the tribal man inevitably divided into two sets of actions, which appeared under two different ethical aspects: the relation within the tribe and the relation with outsiders, the double conception of morality maintaining itself until now. But the tribal law differed no more widely from inter-tribal law than our common law does from our international law. Until society manages to combine the two we shall make no headway toward the Newer Ideals of Peace.

If we would institute an intelligent search for the social conditions which make possible this combination we should naturally seek for them in the poorer quarters of a cosmopolitan city where we have, as

nowhere else, the conditions for breaking into this double development; for making a fresh start, as it were, toward a synthesis upon a
higher moral line which shall include both. There is every opportunity
and necessity for compassion and kindliness such as the tribe itself
afforded, and there is in addition, because of the many nationalities
which are gathered there from all parts of the world, the opportunity
and necessity for breaking through the tribal bond. Early associations
and affections were not based so much on ties of blood as upon that
necessity for defense against the hostile world outside which made the
life of every man in a tribe valuable to every other man. The fact of
blood was, so to speak, an accident. The moral code grew out of solidarity, of emotion and action essential to the life of all.

In the midst of the modern city which, at moments, seems to stand
only for the triumph of the strongest, the successful exploitation of
the weak, the ruthlessness and hidden crime which follow in the wake
of the struggle for existence on its lowest terms, there come daily—at
least to American cities—accretions of simple people, who carry in
their hearts a desire for mere goodness. They regularly deplete their
scanty livelihood in response to a primitive pity, and, independent of
the religions they have professed, of the wrongs they have suffered,
and of the fixed morality they have been taught, have an unquenchable
desire that charity and simple justice shall regulate men's relations. It
seems sometimes, to one who knows them, as if they continually sought
for an outlet for more kindliness, and that they are not only willing
and eager to do a favor for a friend, but that their kindheartedness lies
in ambush, as it were, for a chance to incorporate itself in our larger
relations, that they persistently expect that it shall be given some form
of governmental expression. This is doubtless due partly to the fact
that emotional pity and kindness are always found in greatest degree
among the unsuccessful. We are told that unsuccessful struggle breeds
emotion, not strength; that the hard-pressed races are the emotional
races; and that wherever struggle has long prevailed emotion becomes
the dominant force in fixing social relations. Is it surprising, therefore,
that among this huge mass of the unsuccessful, to be found in certain
quarters of the modern city, we should have the "medium," in which
the first growth of the new compassion is taking place?

In addition to this compassion always found among the unsuccessful, emotional sentiment runs high among the newly arrived immigrants as a result of the emotional experiences of parting from home and kindred, to which he has been so recently subjected. An unusual mental alertness and power of perception also results from the upheaval. The multitudes of immigrants flooding the American cities have many times sundered social habits cherished through a hundred generations, and have renounced customs that may be traded to the habits of primitive man. These old habits and customs have a much more powerful hold than have mere racial or national ties. In seeking companionship in the new world, all the immigrants are reduced to the fundamental equalities and universal necessities of human life itself, and they inevitably develop the power of association which comes from daily contact with those who are unlike each other in all save the universal characteristics of man.

When looked at too closely, this nascent morality disappears, and one can count over only a thousand kindly acts and neighborly offices. But when meditated upon in the whole, there at once emerge again those vast and dominant suggestions of a new peace and holiness. It would seem as if our final help and healing were about to issue forth from broken human nature itself, out of the pathetic striving of ordinary men, who make up the common substance of life: from those who have been driven by economic pressure or governmental oppression out of a score of nations.

These various peoples who are gathered together in the immigrant quarters of a cosmopolitan city worship goodness for its own value, and do not associate it with success any more than they associate success with themselves; they literally "serve God for nought." If we would adduce evidence that we are emerging from a period of industrialism into a period of humanitarianism, it is to such quarters that we must betake ourselves. These are the places in which it is easiest to study the newer manifestations of government, in which personal welfare is considered a legitimate object; for a new history of government begins with an attempt to make life possible and human in large cities, in those crowded quarters which exhibit such an undoubted tendency to barbarism and degeneracy when the better human qualities are not nourished. Public baths and gymnasiums, parks and libraries, are provided first for those who are without the security for bare subsistence, and it does not seem strange to them that it should be so. Such a community is made up of men who will continue to dream of Utopian Governments until the democratic government about them expresses kindliness with protection. Such men will continue to rely upon neighborly friendliness until organized charity is able to identify impulsive pity with well-considered relief. They will naively long for an education for their children that will fit them to earn money until public education shall come to consider industrial efficiency. As their hopes and dreams are a prophecy of the future development in city government, in charity, in education, so their daily lives are a forecast of coming international relations. Our attention has lately been drawn to the fact that it is logical that the most vigorous efforts in governmental reform, as well as the most generous experiments in ministering to social needs, have come from the larger cities and that it is inevitable that they should be to-day "the centers of radicalism," as they have been traditionally the "cradles of liberty."[2]

If we once admit the human dynamic character of progress, then it is easy to understand why the crowded city quarters become focal points of that progress.

A deeper and more thorough-going unity is required in a community made up of highly differentiated peoples than in a more settled and stratified one, and it may be logical that we should find in this commingling of many peoples a certain balance and concord of opposing and contending forces; a gravitation toward the universal. Because of their difference in all external matters, in all of the non-essentials of life, the people in a cosmopolitan city are forced to found their community of interests upon the basic and essential likenesses of their common human nature; for, after all, the things that make men alike are stronger and more primitive than the things that separate them. It is natural that this synthesis of the varying nations should be made first at the points of the greatest congestion, quite as we find that selfishness is first curbed and social feeling created at the points where the conflict of individual interests is sharpest. One dares not grow too certain as to the wells of moral healing which lie under the surface of the sullen work-driven life which the industrial quarters of the modern

2. *The Growth of Cities in the Nineteenth Century*, A. T. Weber, page 432.

city present. They fascinate us by their mere size and diversity, as does the city itself; but certain it is, that these quarters continually confound us by their manifestations of altruism. It may be that we are surprised simply because we fail to comprehend that the individual, under such pressure, must shape his life with some reference to the demands of social justice, not only to avoid crushing the little folk about him, but in order to save himself from death by crushing. It is an instance of the irresistible coalescing of the altruistic and egoistic impulse which is the strength of social morality. We are often told that men under this pressure of life become calloused and cynical, whereas anyone who lives with them knows that they are sentimental and compassionate.

It is possible that we shall be saved from warfare by the "fighting rabble" itself, by the "quarrelsome mob" turned into kindly citizens of the world through the pressure of a cosmopolitan neighborhood. It is not that they are shouting for peace—on the contrary, if they shout at all, they will continue to shout for war—but that they are really attaining cosmopolitan relations through daily experience. They will probably believe for a long time that war is noble and necessary both to engender and cherish patriotism; and yet all of the time, below their shouting, they are living in the kingdom of human kindness. They are laying the simple and inevitable foundations for an international order as the foundations of tribal and national morality have already been laid. They are developing the only sort of patriotism consistent with the intermingling of the nations; for the citizens of a cosmopolitan quarter find an insuperable difficulty when they attempt to hem in their conception of patriotism either to the "old country" or to their adopted one. There arises the hope that when this newer patriotism becomes large enough, it will overcome arbitrary boundaries and soak up the notion of nationalism. We may then give up war, because we shall find it as difficult to make war upon a nation at the other side of the globe as upon our next-door neighbor.

These humble harbingers of the Newer Ideals of Peace, venturing themselves upon a larger relationship, are most touching; and while the success of their efforts can never be guaranteed or spoken of too confidently, they stir us with a strange hope, as if new vistas of life were opening before us—vistas not illuminated with the glare of war, but with a mellowed glow of their own. These paths are seen distinctly only as we ascend to a more enveloping point of view and obtain a larger and bulkier sense of the growing sentiment which rejects the old and negative bonds of discipline and coercion and insists upon vital and fraternal relationship, subordinating the lower to the higher. To make this hope valid and intelligible, is indeed the task before these humble brethren of ours and of those who would help them. They encourage us to hope for the discovery of a new vital relation—that of the individual to the race—which may lay the foundation for a new religious bond adequate to the modern situation; and we almost come to believe that such a foundation is, in fact, being laid now—not in speculation, but in action.

That which secured for the early Hebrew shepherd his health, his peace of mind, and his sense of connection with the Unseen, became the basis for the most wonderful and widespread religion the world has ever known. Perhaps, at this moment, we need to find that which will secure the health, the peace of mind, and the opportunity for normal occupation and spiritual growth to the humblest industrial worker, as the foundation for a rational conduct of life adapted to an industrial and cosmopolitan era.

Even now we only dimly comprehend the strength and irresistible power of those "universal and imperious ideals which are formed in the depths of anonymous life," and which the people insist shall come to realization, not because they have been tested by logic or history, but because the mass of men are eager that they should be tried as a living experience. According to our different methods of viewing society, we express this newer ideal which is after all so old as to have been engendered in the tribe itself. He who makes the study of society a mere corollary of biology, speaks of the "theory of the unspecialized," that the simple cell develops much more rapidly when new tissue is needed than the more highly developed one; he who views society from the economic standpoint and finds hope only in a changed industrial order, talks of the "man at the bottom of society," of the proletarian who shall eventually come into his own; he who believes that a wiser and a saner education will cure our social ill, speaks ever and again of "the wisdom of the little child" and of the necessity to reveal and explore his capacity; while he who keeps close to the historic deductions upon which the study of society is chiefly founded, uses the old religious phrase, "the counsel of imperfection," and bids us concern ourselves with "the least of these."

The French have a phrase *l'imperieuse bonté* by which they designate those impulses towards compassionate conduct which will not be denied, because they are as imperative in their demand for expression as is the impulse to make music or to soften life by poesy and decoration. According to this definition, St. Francis was a genius in exactly the same sense as was Dante or Raphael, and he revealed quite as they did, possibilities and reaches of the human soul hitherto unsuspected. This genius for goodness has in the past largely expressed itself through individuals and groups, but it may be that we are approaching a period which shall give it collective expression, and shall unite into one all those private and parochial efforts. It would be no more strange than was that marvelous coming together of the artists and the people in the thirteenth century which resulted in the building of the Gothic cathedrals. We may be waiting for a religious enthusiasm, for a divine fire to fuse together the partial and feeble efforts at "doing good" into a transfigured whole which shall take on international proportions as naturally as the cathedrals towered into unheard of heights. The Gothic cathedrals were glorious beyond the dreams of artists, notwithstanding that they were built by unknown men, or rather by so many men that it was a matter of indifference to record their names. Could we compare the present humanitarian efforts to the building of a spiritual cathedral, it would seem that the gargoyles had been made first, that the ground is now strewn with efforts to "do good" which have developed a diabolical capacity for doing harm. But even these may fall into place. The old cathedral-builders fearlessly portrayed all of life, its inveterate tendency to deride as well as to bless; its trickery as well as its beauty. Their art was catholic enough to portray all, and the cathedral was huge enough to mellow all they portrayed into a flowing and inspired whole.

At the present moment it requires the philosopher to unify these spiritual efforts of the common man into the internationalism of good will, as in the past it was natural that the philosophers, the men who looked at life as a whole, should have been the first to sigh for negative peace which they declared would be "eternal."

Speculative writers, such as Kant, Bentham, and Buckle, long ago pointed out that the subsidence of war was inevitable as society progressed. They contended that every stage of human progress is marked by a further curtailment of brute force, a limitation of the area in which it is permitted. At the bottom is the small savage community in a perpetual state of warfare; at the top an orderly society stimulated and controlled by recognized ideals of social justice. In proportion as the savage society comes under the dominion of a common moral consciousness, it moves up, and in proportion as the civilized society reverts to the use of brute force, it goes down. Reversion to that brute struggle may at any moment cost the destruction of the painfully acquired bonds of equity, the ties of mutual principle, which are wrought with such effort and loosed with such ease. But these earlier philosophers could not possibly have foreseen the tremendous growth of industry and commerce with their inevitable cosmopolitanism which has so recently taken place, nor without knowledge of this could they possibly have prognosticated the leap forward and the aggressive character which the concern for human welfare has latterly evinced. The speculative writers among our contemporaries are naturally the only ones who formulate this new development, or rather bid us heed its presence among us. An American philosopher[3] has lately reminded us of the need to "discover in the social realm the moral equivalent for war—something heroic that will speak to men as universally as war has done, and yet will be as compatible with their spiritual natures as war has proved itself to be incompatible." It may be true that we are even now discovering these moral substitutes, although we find it so difficult to formulate them. Perhaps our very hope that these substitutes may be discovered has become the custodian of a secret change that is going on all about us. We care less each day for the heroism connected with warfare and destruction, and constantly admire more that which pertains to labor and the nourishing of human life. The new heroism manifests itself at the present moment in a universal determination to abolish poverty and disease, a manifestation so widespread that it may justly be called international.

In illustration of this new determination one immediately thinks of the international effort to rid the face of the earth of tuberculosis, in

3. William James, Professor of Philosophy at Harvard University.

which Germany, Italy, France, England and America are engaged with such enthusiasm. This movement has its international congresses, its discoverers and veterans, also its decorations and rewards for bravery. Its discipline is severe; it requires self-control, endurance, self-sacrifice and constant watchfulness. Its leaders devote hours to careful teaching and demonstration, they reclaim acres of bad houses, and make over the food supply of huge cities. One could instance the determination to do away with neglected old age, which finds expression in the Old Age Pension Acts of Germany and Australia, in the State Savings Banks of Belgium and France, in the enormous number of Mutual Benefit Societies in England and America. In such undertakings as these, with their spontaneous and universal manifestations, are we beginning to see the first timid forward reach of one of those instinctive movements which carry onward the progressive goodness of the race.

It is possible that this substitution of nurture for warfare is analogous to that world-wide effort to put a limit to revenge which one nation after another essayed as each reached a certain stage of development. To compel the avenger to accept blood-money in lieu of the blood of his enemy may have been but a short step in morals, but at least it destroyed the stimulus to further shedding of blood which each avenged death had afforded, and it laid the foundations for court adjudications. The newer humanitarianism is more aggressive and substitutes emotional stimuli as well as codes of conduct. We may predict that each nation quite as a natural process will reach the moment when virile good-will will be substituted for the spirit of warfare. The process of extinguishing war, however, compared to the limiting of revenge, will be amazingly accelerated. Owing to the modern conditions of intercourse, each nation will respond, not to an isolated impulse, but will be caught in the current of a world-wide process.

We are much too timid and apologetic in regard to this newer humanitarianism, and do not yet realize what it may do for us in the way of courage and endurance. We continue to defend war on the ground that it stirs the nobler blood and the higher imagination of the nation, and thus frees it from moral stagnation and the bonds of commercialism. We do not see that this is to borrow our virtues from a former age and to fail to utilize our own. We find ourselves in this plight because our modern morality has lacked fibre, because our humanitarianism has been much too soft and literary, and has given itself over to unreal and high-sounding phrases. It appears that our only hope for a genuine adjustment of our morality and courage to our present social and industrial developments, lies in a patient effort to work it out by daily experience. We must be willing to surrender ourselves to those ideals of the humble, which all religious teachers unite in declaring to be the foundations of a sincere moral life.

The following pages attempt to uncover these newer ideals as we may daily experience them in the modern city. It may be found that certain survivals of militarism in municipal government are responsible for much of the failure in the working of democratic institutions. We may discover that the survivals of warfare in the labor movement and all the other dangers of class morality rest largely upon an appeal to loyalties which are essentially a survival of the virtues of a warlike period. The more aggressive aspects of the newer humanitarianism may be traced in the movement for social amelioration and in the protective legislation which regards the weakest citizen as a valuable asset. The same spirit which protests against the social waste of child labor also demands that the traditional activity of woman shall be utilized in civic life. When the State protects its civic resources, as it formerly defended its citizens in time of war, industrialism versus militarism comes to be nurture versus conquest. In order to trace the displacement of the military ideals of patriotism by those of a rising concern for human welfare, we must take an accounting between those forms of governmental machinery and social organization which are the historic outgrowth of conquest and repression and the newer forms arising in their midst which embody the social energy instantly recognizable as contemporaneous with our sincerest moral life. To follow this newer humanitarianism even through its obvious manifestations requires at the very outset a definite aban-donment of the eighteenth-century philosophy upon which so much of our present democratic theory and philanthropic activity depends. It is necessary from the very beginning to substitute the scientific method of research for the a priori method of the school men if we would deal with real people and obtain a sense of participation with our fellows. The eighteenth-century humanitarian hotly insisted upon "the rights of man," but he loved the people without really knowing them, which is by no means an impossible achievement. "The love of those whom a man does not know is quite as elemental a sentiment as the love of those whom a man does know," but with this difference, that he shuts himself away from the opportunity of being caught and carried forward in the stream of their hopes and aspirations, a bigger and warmer current than he dreams of. The eighteenth-century humanitarian substituted his enthusiastic concept of "the natural man" for the warmth which this stream might have given him, and so long as he dealt with political concepts it answered his purpose. Mazzini made a most significant step between the eighteenth-century morality and our own by appealing beyond "the rights of man" to the "duties to humanity;" but although an impassioned democrat, he was still a moralist of the earlier type. He realized with them that the appeal to humanity would evoke a finer and deeper response than that to patriotism or to any sectional morality; but he shared the eighteenth-century tendency to idealization. It remained for the moralist of this generation to dissolve "humanity" into its component parts of men, women, and children and to serve their humblest needs with an enthusiasm which, so far from being dependent upon glamour, can be sustained only by daily knowledge and constant companionship.

It is no easy task to detect and to follow the tiny paths of progress which the unencumbered proletarian with nothing but his life and capacity for labor, is pointing out for us. These paths lead to a type of government founded upon peace and fellowship as contrasted with restraint and defence. They can never be discovered with the eyes of the doctrinaire. From the nature of the case, he who would walk these paths must walk with the poor and oppressed, and can only approach them through affection and understanding. The ideals of militarism would forever shut him out from this new fellowship.

II

Survivals of Militarism in City Government

✍ We are accustomed to say that the machinery of government incorporated in the charters of the early American cities, as in the Federal and State constitutions, was worked out by men who were strongly under the influence of the historians and doctrinaires of the eighteenth century. The most significant representative of these men is Thomas Jefferson, and their most telling phrase, the familiar opening that "all men are created free and equal."

We are only now beginning to suspect that the present admitted failure in municipal administration, the so-called "shame of American cities," may be largely due to the inadequacy of those eighteenth-century ideals, with the breakdown of the machinery which they provided. We recognize the weakness inherent in the historic and doctrinaire method when it attempts to deal with growing and human institutions. While these men were strongly under the influence of peace ideals which were earnestly advocated, both in France and in America, even in the midst of their revolutionary periods, and while they read the burning poets and philosophers of their remarkable century, their idealism, after all, was largely founded upon theories concerning "the natural man," a creature of their sympathetic imaginations.

Because their idealism was of the type that is afraid of experience, these founders refused to look at the difficulties and blunders which a self-governing people were sure to encounter, and insisted that, if only the people had freedom, they would walk continuously in the paths of justice and righteousness. It was inevitable, therefore, that they should have remained quite untouched by that worldly wisdom which counsels us to know life as it is, and by that very modern belief that if the world is ever to go right at all, it must go right in its own way. A man of this generation easily discerns the crudeness of "that eighteenth-century conception of essentially unprogressive human nature in all the empty dignity of its 'inborn rights.'"[1] Because he has grown familiar with a more passionate human creed, with the modern evolutionary conception of the slowly advancing race whose rights are not "inalienable," but hard-won in the tragic processes of experience, he realizes that these painfully acquired rights must be carefully cherished or they may at any moment slip out of our hands. We know better in America than anywhere else that civilization is not a broad road, with mile-stones indicating how far each nation has proceeded upon it, but a complex struggle forward, each race and nation contributing its quota; that the variety and continuity of this commingled life afford its charm and value. We would not, if we could, conform them to one standard. But this modern attitude, which may even now easily subside into negative tolerance, did not exist among the founders of the Republic, who, with all their fine talk of the "natural man" and what he would accomplish when he obtained freedom and equality, did not really trust the people after all.

They timidly took the English law as their prototype, "whose very root is in the relation between sovereign and subject, between lawmaker and those whom the law restrains," which has traditionally concerned itself more with the guarding of prerogative and with the rights of property than with the spontaneous life of the people. They serenely incorporated laws and survivals which registered the successful struggle of the barons against the aggressions of the sovereign, although the new country lacked both nobles and kings. Misled by the name of government, they founded their new government by an involuntary reference to a lower social state than that which they actually saw about them. They depended upon penalties, coercion, compulsion, remnants of military codes, to hold the community together; and it may be possible to trace much of the maladministration of our cities to these survivals, to the fact that our early democracy was a moral romanticism, rather than a well-grounded belief in social capacity and in the efficiency of the popular will.

---

1. "The Spirit of Modern Philosophy," Josiah Royce, page 275.

It has further happened that as the machinery, groaning under the pressure of new social demands put upon it, has broken down that from time to time, we have mended it by giving more power to administrative officers, because we still distrusted the will of the people. We are willing to cut off the dislocated part or to tighten the gearing, but are afraid to substitute a machine of newer invention and greater capacity. In the hour of danger we revert to the military and legal type although they become less and less appropriate to city life in proportion as the city grows more complex, more varied in resource and more highly organized, and is, therefore, in greater need of a more diffused local autonomy.

A little examination will easily show that in spite of the fine phrases of the founders, the Government became an entity by itself away from the daily life of the people. There was no intention to ignore them nor to oppress them. But simply because its machinery was so largely copied from the traditional European Governments which did distrust the people, the founders failed to provide the vehicle for a vital and genuinely organized expression of the popular will. The founders carefully defined what was germane to government and what was quite outside its realm, whereas the very crux of local self-government, as has been well said, is involved in the "right to locally determine the scope of the local government," in response to the needs as they arise.

They were anxious to keep the reins of government in the hands of the good and professedly public-spirited, because, having staked so much upon the people whom they really knew so little, they became eager that they should appear well, and should not be given enough power to enable them really to betray their weaknesses. This was done in the same spirit in which a kind lady permits herself to give a tramp five cents, believing that, although he may spend it for drink, he cannot get very drunk upon so small a sum. In spite of a vague desire to trust the people, the founders meant to fall back in every crisis upon the old restraints which government has traditionally enlisted in its behalf, and were, perhaps, inevitably influenced by the experiences of the Revolutionary War. Having looked to the sword for independence from oppressive governmental control, they came to regard the sword as an essential part of the government they had succeeded in establishing.

Regarded from the traditional standpoint, government has always needed this force of arms. The king, attempting to control the growing power of the barons as they wrested one privilege after another from him, was obliged to use it constantly; the barons later successfully established themselves in power only to be encroached upon by the growing strength and capital of the merchant class. These are now, in turn, calling upon the troops and militia for aid, as they are shorn of a pittance here and there by the rising power of the proletariat. The imperial, the feudal, the capitalistic forms of society each created by revolt against oppression from above, preserved their own forms of government only by carefully guarding their hardly won charters and constitutions. But in the very countries where these successive social forms have developed, full of survivals of the past, some beneficent and some detrimental, governments are becoming modified more rapidly than in this democracy where we ostensibly threw off traditional governmental oppression only to encase ourselves in a theory of virtuous revolt against oppressive government, which in many instances has proved more binding than the actual oppression itself.

Did the founders cling too hard to that which they had won through persecution, hardship, and finally through a war of revolution? Did these doctrines seem so precious to them that they were determined to tie men up to them as long as possible, and allow them no chance to go on to new devices of government, lest they slight these that had been so hardly won? Did they estimate, not too highly, but by too exclusive a valuation, that which they had secured through the shedding of blood?

Man has ever overestimated the spoils of war, and tended to lose his sense of proportion in regard to their value. He has ever surrounded them with a glamour beyond their deserts. This is quite harmless when the booty is an enemy's sword hung over a household fire, or a battered flag decorating a city hall, but when the spoil of war is an idea which is bound on the forehead of the victor until it cramps his growth, a theory which he cherishes in his bosom until it grows so large and near that it afflicts its possessor with a sort of disease of responsibility for its preservation, it may easily overshadow the very people for whose cause the warrior issued forth.

Was this overestimation of the founders the cause of our subsequent failures? or rather did not the fault lie with their successors, and does it not now rest with us, that we have wrapped our inheritance in a napkin and refused to add thereto? The founders fearlessly took the noblest word of their century and incorporated it into a public document. They ventured their fortunes and the future of their children upon its truth. We, with the belief of a progressive, developing human life, apparently accomplish less than they with their insistence upon rights and liberties which they so vigorously opposed to mediaeval restrictions and obligations. We are in that first period of conversion when we hold a creed which forecasts newer and larger possibilities for governmental development, without in the least understanding its spiritual implications. Although we have scrupulously extended the franchise to the varied immigrants among us, we have not yet admitted them into real political fellowship.

It is easy to demonstrate that we consider our social and political problems almost wholly in the light of one wise group whom we call native Americans, legislating for the members of humbler groups whom we call immigrants. The first embodies the attitude of contempt or, at best, the patronage of the successful towards those who have as yet failed to succeed. We may consider the so-called immigration situation as an illustration of our failure to treat our growing Republic in the spirit of a progressive and developing democracy.

The statement is made many times that we, as a nation, are rapidly reaching the limit of our powers of assimilation, that we receive further masses of immigrants at the risk of blurring those traits and characteristics which we are pleased to call American, with its corollary that the national standard of living is in danger of permanent debasement. Were we not in the midst of a certain intellectual dearth and apathy, of a skepticism in regard to the ideals of self-government which have ceased to charm men, we would see that we are testing our national life by a tradition too provincial and limited to meet its present motley and cosmopolitan character; that we lack mental energy, adequate knowledge, and a sense of the youth of the earth. The constant cry that American institutions are in danger betrays a spiritual waste, not due to our infidelity to national ideals, but arising from the fact that we fail to enlarge those ideals in accord with our faithful experience of life. Our political machinery devised for quite other conditions, has not been readjusted and adapted to the successive changes resulting from our development. The clamor for the town meeting, for the colonial and early century ideals of government is in itself significant, for we are apt to cling to the past through a very paucity of ideas.

In a sense the enormous and unprecedented moving about over the face of the earth on the part of all nations is in itself the result of philosophic dogma of the eighteenth century—of the creed of individual liberty. The modern system of industry and commerce presupposes freedom of occupation, of travel, and residence; even more, it unhappily rests in a large measure upon the assumption of a body of the unemployed and the unskilled, ready to be absorbed or dropped according to the demands of production: but back of that, or certainly preceding its later developments, lies "the natural rights" doctrine of the eighteenth century. Even so late as 1892 an official treaty of the United States referred to the "inalienable rights of man to change his residence and religion." This dogma of the schoolmen, dramatized in France and penetrating under a thousand forms into the most backward European States, is still operating as an obscure force in sending emigrants to America and in our receiving them here. But in the second century of its existence it has become too barren and chilly to induce any really zealous or beneficent activity on behalf of the immigrants after they arrive. On the other hand those things which we do believe—the convictions which might be formulated to the immeasurable benefit of the immigrants, and to the everlasting good of our national life, have not yet been satisfactorily stated, nor apparently apprehended by us, in relation to this field. We have no method by which to discover men, to spiritualize, to understand, to hold intercourse with aliens and to receive of what they bring. A century-old abstraction breaks down before this vigorous test of concrete cases and their demand for sympathetic interpretation. When we are confronted by the Italian lazzaroni, the peasants from the Carpathian foothills, and the proscribed traders from Galatia, we have no national ideality founded upon realism and tested by our growing experience with which to meet them, but only the platitudes of our crudest youth. The philosophers and statesmen of the eighteenth-century believed that the universal franchise would cure all ills; that liberty and equality rested only upon constitutional rights and privileges; that to obtain these two and to throw off all governmental oppression constituted the full duty of the progressive patriot. We still keep to this formalization because the philosophers of this generation give us nothing newer. We ignore the fact that world-wide problems can no longer be solved by a political constitution assuring us against opposition, but that we must frankly face the proposition that the whole situation is more industrial than political. Did we apprehend this, we might then realize that the officers of the Government who are dealing with naturalization papers and testing the knowledge of the immigrants concerning the Constitution of the United States, are only playing with counters representing the beliefs of a century ago, while the real issues are being settled by the great industrial and commercial interests which are at once the products and the masters of our contemporary life. As children who are allowed to amuse themselves with poker chips pay no attention to the real game which their elders play with the genuine cards in their hands, so we shut our eyes to the exploitation and industrial debasement of the immigrant, and say, with placid contentment, that he has been given the rights of an American citizen, and that, therefore, all our obligations have been fulfilled. It is as if we should undertake to cure the contemporary political corruption founded upon a disregard of the Inter-State Commerce Acts, by requiring the recreant citizens to repeat the Constitution of the United States.

As yet no vigorous effort is made to discover how far our present system of naturalization, largely resting upon laws enacted in 1802, is inadequate, although it may have met the requirements of "the fathers." These processes were devised to test new citizens who had immigrated to the United States from political rather than from economic pressure, although these two have always been in a certain sense coextensive. Yet the early Irish came to America to seek an opportunity for self-government, denied them at home; the Germans and Italians started to come in largest numbers after the absorption of their smaller States into the larger nations; and the immigrants from Russia are the conquered Poles, Lithuanians, Finns, and Jews. On some such obscure notion the processes of naturalization were worked out, and, with a certain degree of logic, the first immigrants were presented with the Constitution of the United States as a type and epitome of that which they had come to seek. So far as they now come in search of political liberty, as many of them do every day, the test is still valid, but, in the meantime, we cannot ignore those significant figures which show emigration to rise with periods of depression in given countries, and immigration to be checked by periods of depression in America, and we refuse to see how largely the question has become an economic one.

At the present moment, as we know, the actual importing of immigrants is left largely to the energy of steamship companies and to those agents for contract labor who are keen enough to avoid the restrictive laws. The business man is here again in the saddle, as he so largely is in American affairs. From the time that the immigrants first make the acquaintance of the steamship agent in their own villages, at least until a grandchild is born on the new soil, they are subjected to various processes of exploitation from purely commercial and self-seeking interests. It begins with the representatives of the transatlantic lines and their allies, who convert the peasant holdings into money, and provide the prospective emigrants with needless supplies, such as cartridge belts and bowie knives. The brokers, in manufactured passports, send their clients by successive stages for a thousand miles to a port suiting their purposes. On the way the emigrants' eyes are treated that they may pass the physical test; they are taught to read sufficiently well to meet the literacy test; they are lent enough money to escape the pauper test, and by the time they have reached America, they are so hopelessly in debt that it requires months of work to repay all they have received. During this time they are completely under the control of the last broker in the line, who has his dingy office in an American city. The exploitation continues under the employment agency whose operations verge into those of the politician, through the naturalization henchman, the petty lawyers who foment their quarrels and grievances by the statement that in a free country everybody "goes to law," by the liquor dealers who stimulate a lively trade among them, and, finally, by the lodging-house keepers and the landlords who are not obliged to give them the housing which the American tenant demands. It is a long dreary road, and the immigrant is successfully exploited at each turn. At moments one looking on is driven to quote the Titanic plaint of Walt Whitman:

"As I stand aloof and look, there is to me something profoundly affecting in large masses of men following the lead of those who do not believe in men."

The sinister aspect of this exploitation lies in the fact that it is carried on by agents whose stock in trade are the counters and terms of citizenship. It is said that at the present moment there are more of these agents in Palermo than perhaps in any other European port, and that those politicians who have found it impossible to stay even in that corrupt city are engaged in the brokerage of naturalization papers in the United States. Certainly one effect of the stringent contract labor laws has been to make the padrones more powerful because "smuggled alien labor" has become more valuable to American corporations, and also to make simpler the delivery of immigrant votes according to the dictates of commercial interests. It becomes a veritable system of poisoning the notions of decent government; but because the entire process is carried on in political terms, because the poker chips are colored red, white, and blue, we are childishly indifferent to it. An elaborate avoidance of restrictions quickly adapts itself to changes either in legislation here or at the points of departure, because none of the legislation is founded upon a real analysis of the situation. For instance, a new type of broker in Russia during the Russian-Japanese War made use of the situation in the interests of young Russian Jews. If one of these men leaves the country ordinarily, his family is obliged to pay three hundred rubles to the Government, but if he first joins the army, his family is free from this obligation for he has passed into the keeping of his sergeant. Out of four hundred Russian Jews who, during three months, were drafted into the army at a given recruiting station, only ten reported, the rest having escaped through immigration. Of course the entire undertaking is much more hazardous, because the man is a deserter from the army in addition to his other disabilities; but the brokers merely put up the price of their services and continue their undertakings.

All these evasions of immigration laws and regulations are simply possible because the governmental tests do not belong to the current situation, and because our political ideas are inherited from governmental conditions not our own. In our refusal to face the situation, we have persistently ignored the political ideals of the Celtic, Germanic, Latin, and Slavic immigrants who have successively come to us; and in our overwhelming ambition to remain Anglo-Saxon, we have fallen into the Anglo-Saxon temptation of governing all peoples by one standard. We have failed to work out a democratic government which should include the experiences and hopes of all the varied peoples among us. We justify the situation by some such process as that employed by each English elector who casts a vote for seventy-five subjects besides himself. He indirectly determines—although he may be a narrow-minded trades-man or a country squire interested only in his hounds and horses—the colonial policy, which shall in turn control the destinies of the Egyptian child toiling in the cotton factory in Alexandria, and of the half-starved Parsee working the opium fields of North India. Yet he cannot, in the nature of the case, be informed of the needs of these far-away people and he would venture to attempt it only in regard to people whom he considered "inferior."

Pending a recent election, a Chicago reformer begged his hearers to throw away all selfish thoughts of themselves when they went to the polls and to vote in behalf of the poor and ignorant foreigners of the city. It would be difficult to suggest anything which would result in a more serious confusion than to have each man, without personal knowledge and experiences, consider the interests of the newly arrived immigrant. The voter would have to give himself over to a veritable debauch of altruism in order to persuade himself that his vote would be of the least value to those men of whom he knew so little, and whom he considered so remote and alien to himself. In truth the attitude of the advising reformer was in reality so contemptuous that he had never considered the immigrants really partakers and molders of the politi-cal life of his country.

This attitude of contempt, of provincialism, this survival of the spirit of the conqueror toward an inferior people, has many manifesta-tions, but none so harmful as when it becomes absorbed and imitated and is finally evinced by the children of the foreigners toward their own parents.

We are constantly told of the increase of criminals in the second generation of immigrants, and, day after day, one sees lads of twelve and fourteen throwing off the restraint of family life and striking out for themselves. The break has come thus early, partly from the forced development of the child under city conditions, partly because the par-ents have had no chance of following, even remotely, this development, but largely because the Americanized child has copied the contemptuous attitude towards the foreigner which he sees all about him. The revolt has in it something of the city impatience of country standards, but much more of America against Poland or Italy. It is all wretchedly sordid with bitterness on the part of the parents, and hardhearted indifference and recklessness on the part of the boy. Only occasionally can the latter be appealed to by filial affection after the first break has once been thoroughly made; and yet, sometimes, even these lads see the pathos of the situation. A probation officer from Hull-House one day surprised three truants who were sitting by a bonfire which they had built near the river. Sheltered by an empty freight car, the officer was able to listen to their conversation. The Pole, the Italian, and the Bohemian boys who had broken the law by staying away from school, by building a fire in dangerous proximity to freight cars, and by "swiping" the potatoes which they were roasting, seemed to have settled down into an almost halcyon moment of gentleness and reminiscence. The Italian boy commiserated his parents because they hated the cold and the snow and "couldn't seem to get used to it"; the Pole said that his father missed seeing folks that he knew and was "sore on this country"; the Bohemian lad really grew quite tender about his old grandmother and the "stacks of relations" who came to see her every Sunday in the old country, where, in contrast to her loneliness here, she evidently had been a person of consequence. All of them felt the pathos of the situation, but the predominant note was the cheap contempt of the new American for foreigners, even though they are of his own blood. The weakening of the tie which connects one generation with another may be called the domestic results of the contemptuous attitude. But the social results of the contemptuous attitude are even more serious and nowhere so grave as in the modern city.

Men are there brought together by multitudes in response to the concentration of industry and commerce without bringing with them the natural social and family ties or the guild relationships which distinguished the mediaeval cities and held even so late as the eighteenth century, when the country people came to town in response to the normal and slowly formed ties of domestic service, family affection, and apprenticeship. Men who come to a modern city by immigration break all these older ties and the national bond in addition. There is all the more necessity to develop that cosmopolitan bond which forms their substitute. The immigrants will be ready to adapt themselves to a new and vigorous civic life founded upon the recognition of their needs if the Government which is at present administered in our cities, will only admit that these needs are germane to its functions. The framers of the carefully prepared charters, upon which the cities are founded, did not foresee that after the universal franchise had once been granted, social needs and ideals were bound to enter in as legitimate objects of political action. Neither did these framers realize, on the other hand, that the only people in a democracy who can legitimately become the objects of repressive government, are those people who are too undeveloped to use their liberty or those who have forfeited their right to full citizenship. We have, therefore, a municipal administration in America which concerns itself only grudgingly with the social needs of the people, and is largely reduced to the administration of restrictive measures. The people who come most directly in contact with the executive officials, who are the legitimate objects of their control, are the vicious, who need to be repressed; and the semi-dependent poor, who appeal to them in their dire need; or, for quite the reverse reason, those who are trying to avoid an undue taxation, resenting the fact that they should be made to support a government which, from the nature of the case, is too barren to excite their real enthusiasm.

The instinctive protest against this mechanical method of civic control, with the lack of adjustment between the natural democratic impulse and the fixed external condition, inevitably produces the indifferent citizen, and the so-called "professional politician." The first, because he is not vicious, feels that the real processes of government do not concern him and wishes only to be let alone. The latter easily adapts himself to an illegal avoidance of the external fixed conditions by assuming that these conditions have been settled by doctrinaires who did not in the least understand the people, while he, the politician, makes his appeal beyond the conditions to the real desires of the people themselves. He is thus not only "the people's friend," but their interpreter. It is interesting to note how often simple people refer to "them," meaning the good and great who govern but do not understand, and to "him," meaning the alderman, who represents them in these incomprehensible halls of State, as an ambassador to a foreign country to whose borders they themselves could not possibly penetrate, and whose language they do not speak.

In addition to this difficulty inherent in the difference between the traditional and actual situation, there is another, which constantly arises on the purely administrative side. The traditional governments which the founders had copied, in proceeding by fixed standards to separate the vicious from the good, and then to legislate against the vicious, had enforced these restrictive measures by trained officials, usually with a military background. In a democracy, however, the officers entrusted with the enforcement of this restrictive legislation, if not actually elected by the people themselves, are still the appointments of those thus elected and are, therefore, good-natured men who have made friends by their kindness and social qualities. This is only decreasingly true even in those cities where appointments are made by civil service examinations. The carrying out of repressive legislation, the remnant of a military state of society, in a democracy is at last put into the hands of men who have attained office because of political pull. The repressive measures must be enforced by those sympathizing with the people and belonging to those against whom the measures operate. This anomalous situation produces almost inevitably one result: that the police authorities themselves are turned into allies of vice and crime. This may be illustrated from almost any of the large American cities in the relation existing between the police force and the gambling and other illicit life. The officers are often flatly told that the enforcement of an ordinance which the better element of the city has insisted upon passing, is impossible; that they are expected to control only the robbery and crime that so often associate themselves with vice. As Mr. Wilcox[2] has recently pointed out, public sentiment itself assumes a certain hypocrisy, and in the end we have "the abnormal conditions which are created when vice is protected by the authorities," and in the very worst cases there develops a sort of municipal blackmail in which the administration itself profits by the violation of law. The very governmental agencies which were designed to protect the citizen from vice, foster and protect him in its pursuance because everybody involved is thoroughly confused by the human element in the situation. Further than this, the officer's very kindness and human understanding is that which leads to his downfall, for he is forced to uphold the remnant of a military discipline in a self-governing com-

2. *The American City,* Dr. Delos F. Wilcox, page 200.

munity. It is not remarkable, perhaps, that the police department, the most vigorous survival of militarism to be found in American cities, has always been responsible for the most exaggerated types of civic corruption. It is sad, however, that this corruption has largely been due to the kindliness of the officers and to their lack of military training. There is no doubt that keeping the saloons in lower New York open on Sunday appeared reasonable to the policemen of the East Side force long before it dawned upon the reform administration; and yet, that the policemen allowed themselves to connive at law-breaking, was the beginning of their disgraceful downfall. Because kindness to an enemy may mean death or the annihilation of the army which he guards, all kindness is illicit on the part of the military sentinel on duty; but to bring that code over bodily into a peaceful social state is to break down the morals of both sides, of the enforcer of the ill-adapted law, as well as of those against whom it is so maladroitly directed.

In order to meet this situation, there is almost inevitably developed a politician of the corrupt type so familiar in American cities, the politician who has become successful because he has made friends with the vicious. The semi-criminal, who are constantly brought in contact with administrative government are naturally much interested in its operations. Having much at stake, as a matter of course, they attend the primaries and all the other election processes which so quickly tire the good citizens whose interest in the government is a self-imposed duty. To illustrate: it is a matter of much moment to a gambler whether there is to be a "wide-open town" or not; it means the success or failure of his business; it involves, not only the pleasure, but the livelihood, of all his friends. He naturally attends to the election of the alderman, to the appointment and retention of the policeman. He is found at the caucus "every time," and would be much amused if he were praised for the performance of his civic duty; but, because he and the others who are concerned in semi-illicit business do attend the primaries, the corrupt politician is nominated over and over again.

As this type of politician is successful from his alliance with crime, there also inevitably arises from time to time a so-called reformer who is shocked to discover the state of affairs, the easy partnership between vice and administrative government. He dramatically uncovers the situation and arouses great indignation against it on the part of good citizens. If this indignation is enough, he creates a political fervor which is translated into a claim upon public gratitude. In portraying the evil he is fighting, he does not recognize, or at least does not make clear, all the human kindness upon which it has grown. In his speeches he inevitably offends a popular audience, who know that the evil of corruption exists in all degrees and forms of human weakness, but who also know that these evils are by no means always hideous, and sometimes even are lovable. They resent his over-drawn pictures of vice and of the life of the vicious; their sense of fair play, their deep-rooted desire for charity and justice, are all outraged.

To illustrate from a personal experience: Some years ago a famous New York reformer came to Chicago to tell us of his phenomenal success, his trenchant methods of dealing with the city "gambling-hells," as he chose to call them. He proceeded to describe the criminals of lower New York in terms and phrases which struck at least one of his auditors as sheer blasphemy against our common human nature. I thought of the criminals whom I knew, of the gambler for whom each Saturday I regularly collected his weekly wage of $24.00, keeping $18.00 for his wife and children and giving him $6.00 on Monday morning. His despairing statement, "the thing is growing on me, and I can never give it up," was certainly not the cry of a man living in hell, but of him who, through much tribulation had at least kept the loyal intention. I remembered the three girls who had come to me with a paltry sum of money collected from the pawn and sale of their tawdry finery in order that one of their number might be spared a death in the almshouse and that she might have the wretched comfort during the closing weeks of her life of knowing that, although she was an outcast, she was not a pauper. I recalled the first murderer whom I had ever known, a young man who was singing his baby to sleep and stopped to lay it in its cradle before he rushed downstairs into his father's saloon to scatter the gang of boys who were teasing the old man by giving him English orders. The old man could not understand English and the boys were refusing to pay for the drinks they had consumed, but technically had not ordered.

For one short moment I saw the situation from the point of view of humbler people, who sin often through weakness and passion, but seldom through hardness of heart, and I felt that in a democratic community such sweeping condemnations and conclusions as the speaker was pouring forth could never be accounted for righteousness.

As the policeman who makes terms with vice, and almost inevitably slides into making gain from vice, merely represents the type of politician who is living off the weakness of his fellows, so the over-zealous reformer who exaggerates vice until the public is scared and awestruck, represents the type of politician who is living off the timidity of his fellows. With the lack of civic machinery for simple democratic expression, for a direct dealing with human nature as it is, we seem doomed to one type or the other—corruptionists or anti-crime committees.

And one sort or the other we will continue to have so long as we distrust the very energy of existence, the craving for enjoyment, the pushing of vital forces, the very right of every citizen to be what he is without pretense or assumption of virtue. Too often he does not really admire these virtues, but he imagines them somewhere as a standard adopted by the virtuous whom he does not know. That old Frankenstein, the ideal man of the eighteenth century, is still haunting us, although he never existed save in the brain of the doctrinaire.

This dramatic and feverish triumph of the self-seeker, see-sawing with that of the interested reformer, does more than anything else, perhaps, to keep the American citizen away from the ideals of genuine evolutionary democracy. Whereas repressive government, from the nature of the case, has to do with the wicked who are happily always in a minority in the community, a normal democratic government would naturally have to do with the great majority of the population in their normal relations to each other.

After all, the so-called "slum politician" ventures his success upon an appeal to human sentiment and generosity. This venture often results in an alliance between the popular politician and the humblest citizens, quite as naturally as the reformer who stands for honest business administration usually becomes allied with the type of business man whose chief concern it is to guard his treasure and to prevent a rise in taxation. The community is again insensibly divided into two camps, the repressed, who is dimly conscious that he has no adequate outlet for his normal life and the repressive, represented by the cautious, careful citizen holding fast to his own,—once more the conqueror and his humble people.

III

Failure to Utilize Immigrants
in City Government

  We do much loose talking in regard to American immigration; we use the phrase, "the scum of Europe," and other unwarranted words without realizing that the unsuccessful man, the undeveloped peasant, may be much more valuable to us here than the more highly developed, but also more highly specialized, town dweller, who may much less readily acquire the characteristics which the new environment demands.

If successful struggle ends in the survival of the few, in blatant and tangible success for the few only, government will have to reckon most largely with the men who have been beaten in the struggle, with the effect upon them of the contest and the defeat; for, after all, the unsuccessful will always represent the majority of the citizens, and it is with the large majority that self-government must eventually deal whatever course of action other governments may legitimately determine for themselves.

To demand to be protected from the many unsuccessful among us, who are supposed to issue forth from the shallows of our city life and seize upon the treasure of the citizens as the barbarians of old came from outside the city walls, is of course not to have read the first lesson of self-government in the light of evolutionary science. It is to forget that a revival in self-government, an awakening of its original motive power and *raison d'être* can come only from a genuine desire to increase its scope, and to adapt it to new and strenuous conditions. In this way science revived and leaped forward under the pressure of the enlarged demand of manufacture and commerce put upon it during the industrial decades just passed.

We would ask the moralists and statesmen of this dawning century, equipped as they are, with the historic method, to save our contemporaries from skepticism in regard to self-government by revealing to them its adaptability to the needs of the humblest man who is so sorely pressed in this industrial age. The statesman who would fill his countrymen with enthusiasm for democratic government must not only possess a genuine understanding of the needs of the simplest citizens, but he must know how to reveal their capacities and powers. He must needs go man-hunting into those curious groups we call newly arrived immigrants, and do for them what the scholar has done in pointing out to us the sweetness and charm which inhere in primitive domestic customs and in showing us the curious pivot these customs make for religious and tribal beliefs. The scholar who has surrounded the simplest action of women grinding millet or corn with a penetrating reminiscence, sweeter than the chant they sing, may reveal something of the same reminiscence and charm among many of the immigrants. In the midst of crowded city streets one stumbles upon an old Italian peasant with her distaff against her withered face and her pathetic hands patiently "holding the thread," as has been done by myriads of women since children needed to be clad; or one sees an old German potter, misshapen by years, his sensitive hands nevertheless fairly alive with skill and delicacy, and his life at least illumined with the artist's prerogative of direct creation. Could we take these primitive habits as they are to be found every day in American cities and give them their significance and place, they would be a wonderful factor for poetry in cities frankly given over to industrialism and absorbed in its activities. As a McAndrews' hymn expresses the frantic rush of the industrial river, so these primitive customs could give us something of the mysticism and charm of the industrial springs, a suggestion of source, a touch of the refinement which adheres to simple things. This study of origins, of survivals, of paths of least resistance—refining an industrial age through the people and experiences which really belong to it and do not need to be brought in from the outside—would surely result in a revived enthusiasm for human life and its possibilities which would in turn react upon the ideals of government. The present lack of understanding of simple people and the dearth of the illumination which knowledge of them would give, can be traced not only in the social and political maladjustment of the immigrant in municipal centres, but is felt in so-called "practical affairs" of national magnitude. Regret is many times expressed that, notwithstanding the fact that nine out of every ten immigrants are of rural birth and are fitted to undertake that painstaking method of cultivating the soil which American farmers despise, they nevertheless all tend to congregate in cities where their inherited and elaborate knowledge of agricultural processes is unutilized. But it is characteristic of American complacency when any assisted removal to agricultural regions is contemplated, that we utterly ignore the past experiences of the immigrant and always assume that each family will be content to live in the middle of its own piece of ground, although there are few peoples on the face of the earth who have ever tried isolating a family on one hundred and sixty acres or on eighty, or even on forty. But this is the American way—a survival of our pioneer days—and we refuse to modify it, even in regard to South Italians, although from the day of mediaeval incursions they have lived in compact villages with an intense and elaborated social life, so much of it out of doors and interdependent that it has affected almost every domestic habit. Italian women knead their own bread, but depend on the village oven for its baking, and the men would rather walk for miles to their fields each day than to face an evening of companionship limited to the family. Nothing could afford a better check to the constant removal to the cities of the farming population all over the United States than the possibility of combining community life with agricultural occupation. This combination would afford that development of civilization which, curiously enough, density alone brings and for which even a free system of rural delivery is not an adequate substitute. Much of the significance and charm of rural life in South Italy lies in its village companionship, quite as the dreariness of the American farm life inheres in its unnecessary solitude. But we totally disregard the solution which the old agricultural community offers, and our utter lack of adaptability has something to do with the fact that the South Italian remains in the city where he soon forgets his cunning in regard to silk worms and olive trees, but continues his old social habits to the extent of filling an entire tenement house with the people from one village.

We also exhibit all the Anglo-Saxon distrust of any experiment with land tenure or method of taxation, although our single-tax advocates do not fail to tell us daily of the stupidity of the present arrangement. It might, indeed, be well to make a few experiments upon an historic basis before their enthusiasm converts us all. For centuries in Russia the Slavic village, the mir system of land occupation, has been in successful operation, training men within its narrow limits to community administration. Yet when a persecuted sect from Russia wishes to find refuge in America, we insist that seven thousand people shall give up all at once a system of land ownership in which they are experts. Americans declare the system to be impracticable, although it is singularly like that in vogue in Palestine during the period of its highest prosperity. We cannot receive them in the United States, because our laws have no way of dealing with such cases. And in Canada, where they are finally settled, the unimaginative Dominion officials are driven to the verge of distraction concerning registration of deeds and the collection of taxes from men who do not claim acres in their own names, but in the name of the village. The official distraction is reflected and intensified among the people themselves, to the point of driving them into the mediaeval "marching mania," in the hope of finding a land in the south where they may carry out their inoffensive "mir" system. The entire situation might prove that an unbending theory of individualism may become as fixed as status itself, although there are certainly other factors in the Doukhobor situation—religious bigotry, and the self-seeking of leadership. In spite of the fact that the Canadian officials have in other matters exhibited much of the adaptability which distinguishes the British colonial policy, they are completely stranded on the rock of Anglo-Saxon individualistic ownership, and assume that any other system of land tenure is subversive of government, forgetting that Russia manages to exert a fair amount of governmental control over thousands of acres held under the system which they so detest.

In our eagerness to reproach the immigrants for not going upon the land we almost overlook the contributions to city life which those of them, who were adapted to it in Europe, are making to our cities here. From dingy little eating-houses in lower New York, performing a function somewhat between the eighteenth-century coffee-house and the Parisian café, is issuing at the present moment perhaps the sturdiest realistic drama that is being produced on American soil. Late into the night speculation is carried forward—not on the nice questions of the Talmud and on quibbles of logic; but minds long trained on these seriously discuss the need of a readjustment of the industrial machine in order that the primitive sense of justice and righteousness may secure larger play in our social organization. And yet a Russian in Chicago who used to believe that Americans cared first and foremost for political liberty and that they would certainly admire those who had suffered in its cause, finds no one interested in his story of six years' banishment beyond the Antarctic [sic] circle. He is really listened to only when he tells the tale to a sportsman of the fish he had caught during the six weeks of summer when the rivers were open. "Lively work then, but plenty of time to eat them dried or frozen through the rest of the year," is the most sympathetic comment he has yet received upon an experience which, at least to him, held the bittersweet of martyrdom.

Among the colonies of the most recently immigrated Jews, who still carry out their orthodox customs and a ritual preserved through centuries in the Ghetto, one constantly feels during a season of religious observance, a refreshing insistence upon the reality of the inner life, and upon the dignity of its expression in inherited form. Perhaps the most striking reproach to the materialism of Chicago is the sight on a solemn Jewish holiday of a Chicago River bridge lined with men and women oblivious of the noisy traffic and sordid surroundings, casting their sins upon the waters that they may be carried far away. The scene is a clear statement that, after all, life does not consist in wealth, in learning, in enterprise, in energy, in success, not even in that modern fetich, culture, but in an inner equilibrium, in "the agreement of soul." It is a relief to see even this exaggerated and grotesque presentation of spiritual values.

But the statesman shuts himself away from the possibility of using these great reservoirs of human ability and motive power because he considers it patriotic to hold to governmental lines and ideals laid down a century and a quarter ago. Because of a military inheritance, we as a nation stoutly contend that all this varied and suggestive life has nothing to do with government nor patriotism, and that we perform the full duty of American citizens when the provisions of the statutes on naturalization are carried out. In the meantime, in the interests of our theory that commercial and governmental powers should have no connection with each other, we carefully ignore the one million false naturalization papers in the United States issued and concealed by commercialized politics. Although we have an uneasy knowledge that these powers are curiously allied, we profess that the latter has no connection with the former and no control over it. We steadily refuse to recognize the fact that our age is swayed by industrial forces.

Fortunately, life is much bigger and finer than our theories about it, and, among all the immigrants in the great cities, there is slowly developing the beginnings of self-government on the lines of their daily experiences. The man who really knows immigrants and undertakes to naturalize them, makes no pretense of the lack of connection between their desire to earn their daily bread and their citizenship. The petty and often corrupt politician who is first kind to immigrants, realizes perfectly well that the force pushing them to this country has been industrial need and that recognition of this need is legitimate. He follows the natural course of events when he promises to get the immigrant "a job," for that is undoubtedly what the immigrant most needs in all the world. If the politician nearest to him were really interested in the immigrant and were to work out a scheme of naturalization fitted to the situation, the immigrant would proceed from the street-cleaning and sewer-digging in which he first engages, to an understanding of the relation of these simple offices to city government. Through them he would understand the obligation of his alderman to secure cleanliness for the streets in which his children play and for the tenement in which he lives. The notion of representative government could be made quite clear and concrete to him. He could demand his rights and use his vote in order to secure them. His very naïve demands might easily become a restraint, a purifying check upon the alderman, instead of a source of constant corruption and exploitation. But when the politician attempts to naturalize the bewildered immigrant, he must perforce accept the doctrinaire standard imposed by men who held a theory totally unattached to experience, and he must, therefore, begin with the remote Constitution of the United States. At the Cook County Court-House only a short time ago a candidate for naturalization, who was asked the usual question as to what the Constitution of the United States was, replied: "The Illinois Central." His mind naturally turned to his work, to the one bit of contribution he had genuinely made to the new country, and his reply might well offer a valuable suggestion to the student of educational method. Some of our most advanced schools are even now making industrial construction and evolution a natural basis for all future acquisition of knowledge, and they claim that anything less vital and creative is inadequate.

It is surprising how a simple experience, if it be but genuine, gives an opening into citizenship altogether lacking to the more grandiose attempts. A Greek-American, slaughtering sheep in a tenement-house yard, reminiscent of the Homeric tradition, can be made to see the effect of the improvised shambles on his neighbor's health and the right of the city to prohibit the slaughtering, only as he perceives the development of city government upon its most modern basis.

The enforcement of adequate child labor laws offers unending opportunity to better citizenship founded, not upon theory but on action, as does the compulsory education law, which makes clear that education is a matter of vital importance to the American city and to the State which has enacted definite, well-considered legislation in regard to it. Some of the most enthusiastic supporters of child-labor legislation and of compulsory education laws are those parents who sacrifice old-world tradition, as well as the much-needed earnings of their young children, because of loyalty to the laws of their adopted country. Certainly genuine sacrifice for the nation's law is a good foundation for patriotism, and as this again is not a doctrinaire question, women are not debarred, and mothers who wash and scrub for the meagre support of their children say, sturdily, sometimes: "It will be a year before he can go to work without breaking the law, but we came to this country to give the young ones a chance, and we are not going to begin by having them do what's not right."

Upon some such basis as this the Hebrew Alliance and the Charity Organization of New York, which are putting forth desperate energy in the enormous task of ministering to the suffering which immigration entails, are developing understanding and respect for the alien through their mutual efforts to secure more adequate tenement-house regulation and to control the spread of tuberculosis; both these undertakings being perfectly hopeless without the intelligent co-operation of the immigrants themselves. Through such humble doors, perchance, the immigrant will at last enter into his heritage in a new nation. Democratic government has ever been the result of spiritual travail and moral effort. Apparently, even here, the immigrant must pay the old cost, and he seems to represent the group and type which is making the most genuine contribution to the present growth in governmental functions, with its constant demand for increasing adaptations.

In the induction of the adult immigrant into practical citizenship, we constantly ignore his daily experience. We also assume in our formal attempts to teach patriotism to him and to his children, that experience and traditions have no value, and that a new sentiment must be put into aliens by some external process. Some years ago, a public-spirited organization engaged a number of speakers to go to the various city schools in order to instruct the children in the significance of Decoration Day and to foster patriotism among the foreign born, by descriptions of the Civil War. In one of the schools, filled with Italian children, an old soldier, a veteran in years and experience, gave a description of a battle in Tennessee, and of his personal adventures in using a pile of brush as an ambuscade and a fortification. Coming from the schoolhouse, an eager young Italian broke out, with characteristic vividness, into a description of his father's campaigning under the leadership of Garibaldi, possibly from some obscure notion that that, too, was a civil war fought from principle, but more likely because the description of one battle had roused in his mind the memory of another such description. The lecturer, whose sympathies happened to be on the other side of the Garibaldian conflict, somewhat sharply told him that he must forget all that; that he was no longer an Italian, but an American. The natural growth of patriotism based upon respect for the achievements of one's fathers, the bringing together of the past with the present, the significance of the almost world-wide effort at a higher standard of political freedom which swept over all Europe and America between 1848 and 1872 could, of course, have no place in the boy's mind because it had none in the mind of the instructor whose patriotism apparently tried to purify itself by the American process of elimination.

How far a certain cosmopolitan humanitarianism ignoring national differences, is either possible or desirable, it is difficult to state; but certain it is that the old type of patriotism, founded upon a common national history and land occupation, becomes to many of the immigrants who bring it with them a veritable stumbling-block and impediment. Many

Greeks whom I know are fairly besotted with a consciousness of their national importance, and the achievements of their glorious past. Among them the usual effort to found a new patriotism upon American history is often an absurd undertaking; for instance, on the night of one Thanksgiving Day, I spent some time and zeal in a description of the Pilgrim Fathers, and the motives which had driven them across the sea, while the experiences of the Plymouth colony were illustrated by stereopticon slides and little dramatic scenes. The audience of Greeks listened respectfully, although I was uneasily conscious of the somewhat feeble attempt to boast of Anglo-Saxon achievement in hardihood and privation, to men whose powers of admiration were absorbed in their Greek background of philosophy and beauty. At any rate, after the lecture was over, one of the Greeks said to me, quite simply, "I wish I could describe my ancestors to you; they were very different from yours." His further remarks were translated by a little Irish boy of eleven, who speaks modern Greek with facility and turns many an honest penny by translating, into the somewhat pert statement: "He says if *that* is what your ancestors are like, that his could beat them out." It is a good illustration of our faculty for ignoring the past, and of our failure to understand the immigrant's estimation of ourselves. This lack of a more cosmopolitan standard, of a consciousness of kind founded upon creative imagination and historic knowledge is apparent in many directions, and cruelly widens the gulf between immigrant fathers and their children who are "Americans in process."

A hideous story comes from New York of a young Russian Jewess who was employed as a stenographer in a down-town office, where she became engaged to be married to a young man of Jewish-American parentage. She felt keenly the difference between him and her newly immigrated parents, and on the night when he was to be presented to them she went home early to make every possible preparation for his coming. Her efforts to make the *ménage* presentable were so discouraging, the whole situation filled her with such chagrin, that an hour before his expected arrival, she ended her life. Although the father was a Talmud scholar of standing in his native Russian town, and the lover was a clerk of very superficial attainments, she possessed no standard by which to judge the two men. This lack of standard must be charged to the entire community; for why should we expect an untrained girl to be able to do for herself what the community so pitifully fails to accomplish? All the members of the community are equally stupid in throwing away the immigrant revelation of social customs and inherited energy. We continually allow this valuable human experience to go to waste although we have reached the stage of humanitarianism when no infant may be wantonly allowed to die, no man be permitted to freeze or starve, if the State can prevent it. We may truthfully boast that the primitive, wasteful struggle of physical existence is practically over, but no such statement can be made in regard to spiritual life. Students of social conditions recognize the fact that modern charity constantly grows more democratic and constructive, and daily more concerned for preventive measures, but to admit frankly similar aims as matters for municipal government as yet seems impossible.

In this country it seems to be only the politician at the bottom, the man nearest the people, who understands that there is a growing disinterestedness taking hold of men's hopes and imaginations in every direction. He often plays upon it and betrays it; but he at least knows it is there.

The two points at which government is developing most rapidly at the present moment are naturally the two where it of necessity exercises functions of nurture and protection: first, in relation to the young criminal, second, in relation to the poor and dependent. One of the latest developments is the Juvenile Courts which the large cities are inaugurating. Only fifteen years ago when I first went to live in an industrial district of Chicago, if a boy was arrested on some trifling charge—and dozens of them were thus arrested each month—the only possible way to secure another chance for him by restoring him to his home with an opportunity to become a law-abiding citizen, was through the alderman of the ward. Upon the request of a distracted relative or the precinct captain, the alderman would "speak to the judge" and secure the release of the boy. The kindness of the alderman was genuine, as was the gratitude of all concerned; but the inevitable impression remained that government was harsh, and naturally dealt out policemen and prisons, and that the political friend alone stood for kindness. That this kindness was in a measure illicit and mysterious in its workings made it all the more impressive.

But so much advance has been made in so short a time as fifteen years, toward incorporating kindly concern for the young and a desire to keep them in the path of rectitude within the process of government itself, that in Chicago alone twenty-four probation officers, as they are called, are paid from the public funds. The wayward boy is committed to one of these for another chance as a part of the procedure of the court. He is not merely released by an act of clemency so magnificent and irrelevant as to dazzle him with a sense of the aldermanic power, but he is put under the actual care of a probation officer that he may do better. He is assisted to keep permanently away from the police courts and their allied penal institutions.

In one of the most successful of these courts, that of Denver, the Judge who can point to a remarkable record with the bad boys of the city, plays a veritable game with them against the police force, he and the boys undertaking to be good without the help of repression, and in spite of the machinations of the police. For instance, if the boys who have been sentenced to the State Reform School at Golden, deliver themselves without the aid of the Sheriff whose duty it is to take them there, they not only vindicate their manliness and readiness "to take their medicine," but they beat the sheriff who belongs to the penal machinery out of his five-dollar fee. Over this fact they openly triumph—a simple example, perhaps, but significant of the attitude of the well-intentioned toward repressive government.

The Juvenile Courts are beginning to take a really parental attitude towards all dependent children, although for years only those orphans who had inherited at least a meagre property were handed over to a public guardian. Those whose parents had left them absolutely nothing were allowed to care for themselves—as if the whole body of doctrine contained in the phrase, "there is no wealth but life," had never entered into the mind of man. Because these courts are dealing with the children in their social and everyday relations they have made the astounding discovery that even a penniless child needs the care and defense of the State.

The schools for Reform are those which are inaugurating the most advanced education in agriculture and manual arts. A bewildered foreign parent comes from time to time to Hull-House, asking that his boy be sent to a school to learn farming, basing his request upon the fact that his neighbor's boy has been sent to "a nice green, country-place." It is carefully explained that the neighbor's boy was bad, and was arrested and sent away because of his badness. After much conversation, the disappointed parent sometimes understands, but he often goes away shaking his head, and some such words as these issue: "I have been in this country for five years, and have never gotten anything yet." At other times it is successfully explained to the man that the city assumes that he is looking out for himself and taking care of his own boy, but it ought to be possible to make him to see that if he feels that his son needs the education of a farm school, that it lies with him to agitate the subject and to vote for the man who will secure such schools. He might well look amazed, were this advice tendered him, for these questions have never been presented to him to vote upon. Because he does not eagerly discuss the tariff or other remote subjects which the political parties present to him from time to time we assume that he is not to be trusted to vote on the education of his child, although there is no doubt that the one thing his ancestors decided upon, from the days of bows and arrows, was the sort of training each one should give his son.

The fine education that is given to a juvenile offender may indicate a certain compunction on the part of the State. Quite as men formerly gloried in warfare and now apologize for it, as they formerly went out to spoil their enemies and now go to civilize them, so civil governments, while continuing to maintain prisons, have become more or less ashamed of them, and are already experimenting in better ways to elevate and reform criminals than by the way of violence and imprisonment. We have already said in America that neither a gallows nor an unmitigated prison shall ever exist for a child.

In the matter of public charities, also, we are not timid as to extending the function of the government. We build enormous city hospitals and almhouses; we care with tenderness for the defective and the dependent; but for that great mass of people just beyond the line, from whom they are constantly recruited, we do practically nothing. It has been said that if a workingman in New York falls a victim to pneumonia, he is taken to a hospital and given skilled treatment; if it leaves him tubercular the city will have a care over him, and valiantly will stand by, putting him into a public sanatorium, providing him with nutritious food and fresh air until his recovery. But if he is turned away from the hospital without tuberculosis, merely too depleted and wretched to go back to his regular employment, then the city can do nothing for him unless he be ready to call himself an out-and-out pauper. We are afraid of the notion of governmental function which would minister to the primitive needs of the mass of the people, although we are quite ready to care for him whom misfortune or disease has made the exception. It is really the rank and file, the average citizen, who is ignored by the government, while he works out his real problems through other agencies, although he is scolded for staying at home on election day, and for refusing to be interested in issues which really do not concern him.

It is comparatively easy to understand the punitive point of view which seeks to suppress, or the philanthropic which seeks to palliate; but it is much more difficult to formulate that city government which is adapted to our present normal living. As over against the survivals of the first two, excellent and necessary as they are, we have but the few public parks and baths, the few band concerts and recreation piers—always excepting, of course, the public schools and the social activities slowly centering around them; for public education has long been a passion in America, and we seem to have been willing to make that an exception to our general theory of government.

While governmental functions have shown this remarkable adaptation and growth in relation to the youth, whether he be in the public schools, in the Juvenile Court or in the reformatory, we hesitate to assume toward the adult this temper of the educator who humbly follows and at the same confidently leads the little child. While the State spends millions of dollars and employs thousands of servants to nurture and heal the sick and defective, it steadfastly refuses to extend its kindliness to the normal working man. The Socialists alone constantly appeal for this extension. They refuse, however, to deal with the present State and constantly take refuge in the formulae of a new scholasticism. Their orators are busily engaged in establishing two substitutes for human nature which they call "proletarian" and "capitalist." They ignore the fact that varying, imperfect human nature is incalculable, and that to eliminate its varied and constantly changing elements is to face all the mistakes and miscalculations which gathered around the "fallen man," or the "economic man," or any other of the fixed norms which have from time to time been substituted for expanding and developing human life. In time "the proletarian" and "the capitalist" will become the impedimenta which it will be necessary to clear away in order to make room for the mass of living and breathing citizens with whom self-government must eventually deal.

There is no doubt that the existence of the mass, the mere size of the modern city, increases the difficulty of the situation. Charles Booth's maps portraying the standard of living for the people of London afford almost the only attempt at a general social survey of a modern city, at least so far as it may be predetermined from the standard of income. From his accompanying twelve volumes may be deduced the occupations of the people, with their real wages, their family budget and their culture level, and, to a certain extent, their recreations and spiritual life. If one gives one's self over to a moment of musing on this mass of information, so huge and so accurate, one is almost instinctively aware that any radical changes, so much needed in the blackest districts, must largely come from forces outside the life of the people. An enlarged mental life must come from the educationalist, increased wages from the business interests, alleviation of suffering from the philanthropists. What vehicle of correction is provided for the people themselves, what device has been invented for loosing that kindliness and mutual aid which is the marvel of all charity visitors? What broad basis has been laid down for a modification of their most genuine and pressing needs through their own initiative? The traditional Government expresses its activity in keeping the streets clean and the district lighted and policed. It is only during the last quarter of a century that the London County Council has erected decent houses, public baths, and many other devices for the purer social life of the people. American cities have gone no further, although they presumably started at workingmen's representation a hundred years ago, so completely were the founders misled by the name of government, and the temptation to substitute the form of political democracy for real self-government dealing with advancing social ideals. Even now London has twenty-eight Borough Councils, in addition to the London County Council itself, fifteen hundred direct representatives of the people, as over against seventy in Chicago although the latter city has a population one-half as large. Paris has twenty Mayors, with corresponding machinery for local government, as over against the New York concentration in one huge City Hall, too often corrupt.

In Germany, perhaps more than anywhere else, the government has come to concern itself with the primitive essential needs of its working-people. In their behalf, the Government has forced industry, in the person of the large manufacturers, to make an alliance with it. The manufacturers are taxed for accident insurance of workingmen, for old-age pensions and sick benefits; and a project is being formed in which they shall bear the large share of insurance against non-employment when it has been made clear that non-employment is the result of an economic crisis brought about through the mal-administration of finance.

Germany proposes to regulate the maximum amount of rent which landlords of certain types of houses may be permitted to require, quite as the usury laws limit the maximum amount of interest which may be demanded. And yet industry in Germany has flourished, and this control on behalf of the normal workingman as he faces life in his daily vocation has apparently not checked its systematic growth, nor limited its place in the world's market. As a result of this constant supervision of industry, the German police although a part of a military government, are constantly employed in the regulation of social affairs; and in these branches of government it is remarked that they are dropping their military tone and assuming toward the people the attitude of helpers and protectors. The police force in Germany is the lowest executive organ of the interior government and there are, therefore, as many kinds of police departments as there are different departments in this interior government. They follow the Government inspectors of the forest, the railways, the fields and roads, to see that their instructions are obeyed. In the Department of Public Health it is the police officers who finally enforce instructions in regard to vaccination, meat inspection, sale of food-stuffs, and the transportation of animals; in the department of factory inspection the police not only enforce the provisions of the factory laws, but they are responsible for the books in which the wages paid to minors are recorded; and it is from the police stations that the cards of the Government insurance for working-people are issued. Any special investigation ordered by the legislature is, as a matter of course, undertaken by the police.

These varied activities, of course, require men of education and ability, and the very extension of function has broken down the military ideal in the country where that ideal is most firmly intrenched. But in a Republic founded upon a revulsion from oppressive government we still keep the police close to their negative role of preserving order and arresting the criminal. The varied functions they perform in Germany would be impossible in America, because it would be hotly resented by the American business man who will not brook any governmental interference in industrial affairs. The inherited instinct that government is naturally oppressive, and that its inroads must be checked, has made it a matter of principle and patriotism to keep the functions of government more restricted and more military than has become true in military countries.

Almost every Sunday in the Italian quarter in which I live various mutual benefit societies march with fife and drum and with a brave showing of banners, celebrating their achievement in having surrounded themselves by at least a thin wall of protection against disaster, upon having set up their mutual good will against the day of misfortune. These parades have all the emblems of patriotism; indeed, the associations present the primitive core of patriotism, brothers standing by each other against hostile forces from without. I assure you that no Fourth of July celebration, no rejoicing over the birth of an heir to the Italian throne, equals in heartiness and sincerity these simple celebrations. Again one longs to pour into the government of their adopted country all this affection and zeal, this real patriotism. A system of State insurance would be a very simple device and secure a large return.

Are we in America retaining eighteenth-century traditions, while Germany is gradually evolving into a Government logically fitted to cope with the industrial situation of the twentieth century? Do we so fail to apprehend what democracy is, that we are really afraid to extend the functions of municipal administration? Have we lost that most conservative of all beliefs—the belief in the average man, and thereby forfeited Aristotle's ideal of a city "where men live a common life for noble ends"?

IV

Militarism and Industrial Legislation

✍ American cities have been slow to consider industrial questions as germane to government, and the Federal authorities have persistently treated the millions of immigrants who arrive every year upon a political theory and method adopted a century ago, because both of them ignore the fact that the organization of industry has completed a revolution during that period. The gigantic task of standardizing the successive nations of immigrants throughout the country has fallen upon workmen because they alone cannot ignore the actual industrial situation. To thousands of workmen the immigration problem is a question of holding a job against a constantly lowering standard of living, and to withstand this stream of "raw labor" means to them the maintenance of industrial efficiency and of life itself. Workingmen are engaged in a desperate struggle to maintain a standard of wages against the constant arrival of unskilled immigrants at the rate of three-quarters of a million a year, at the very period when the elaboration of machinery permits the largest use of unskilled men.

It may be owing to the fact that the workingman is brought into direct contact with the situation as a desperate problem of a living wage against starvation; it may be that wisdom is at her old trick of residing in the hearts of the simple, or that this new idealism, which is that of a reasonable life and labor, must, from the very nature of things, proceed from those who labor; or possibly it may be because amelioration arises whence it is so sorely needed; but certainly it is true, that, while the rest of the country talks of assimilation as if it were a huge digestive apparatus, the man with whom the immigrant has come most sharply into competition, has been forced into fraternal relations with him.

Curiously enough, however, as soon as the immigrant situation is frankly regarded as an industrial one, as these men must regard it, the political aspects of the industrial situation is revealed in the fact that trade organizations which openly concern themselves with the immigration problem on its industrial side, quickly take on the paraphernalia and machinery which have hitherto associated themselves only with governmental life and control. The trades unions have worked out all over again local autonomy, with central councils and national representative bodies and the use of the referendum vote; and they also exhibit many of the features of political corruption and manipulation.

The first real lesson in self-government to many immigrants has come through the organization of labor unions, and it could come in no other way, for the union alone has appealed to their necessities. One sees the first indication of an idealism arising out of these primal necessities, and at moments one dares to hope that it may be sturdy enough and sufficiently founded upon experience to make some impression upon the tremendous immigration situation.

The movements embodying a new idealism have traditionally sought refuge with those who are near to starvation. Although the spiritual struggle is associated with the solitary garret of the impassioned dreamer, it may be that the idealism fitted to our industrial democracy will be evolved in crowded sewer ditches and in noisy factories. It may be contended that this remarkable coming together of the workingman and the immigrant has been the result of an economic pressure, and is without merit or idealism, and that the trades union record on Chinese exclusion and negro discrimination has been damaging. Be that as it may, this assimilation between the immigrant and the workingman has exhibited amazing strength, which may be illustrated from two careful studies made in two different parts of the country.

To quote first from a study made from the University of Wisconsin of the stock yards strike which took place in Chicago in 1904:[1] "Perhaps

1. *Trade Unionism and Labor Problems*, by John R. Commons, page 248.

the fact of the greatest social significance is that this was not merely a strike of skilled labor for the unskilled, but was a strike of American-ized Irish, Germans, and Bohemians, in behalf of Slovaks, Poles, and Lithuanians. . . . This substitution of races in the stock yards has been a continuing process for twenty years. The older nationalities have already disappeared from the unskilled occupations, and the substitu-tion of races has evidently run along the line of lower standard of liv-ing. The latest arrivals, the Lithuanians and Slovaks, are probably the most oppressed of the peasants of Europe." The visitors who attended the crowded meetings of the strikers during the summer of 1904 and heard the same address successively translated by interpreters into six or eight languages, who saw the respect shown to the most uncouth of the speakers by the skilled American men representing a distinctly superior standard of life and thought, could never doubt the power of the labor organizations for amalgamation, whatever opinion they might hold concerning their other values. This may be said in spite of the fact that great industrial disturbances have arisen from the under-cutting of wages by the lowering of racial standard. Certainly the most notable of these have taken place in those industries and at those places in which the importation of immigrants has been deliberately fostered as a wage-lowering weapon; and even in those disturbances and under the shock and strain of a long strike, disintegration did not come along the line of race cleavage.

The other study was made in the anthracite coal fields, and was undertaken from the University of Pennsylvania:[2] "The United Mine Workers of America is taking men of a score of nationalities, English-speaking and Slav, men of widely different creeds, languages, and cus-toms, and of varying powers of industrial competition and is weld-ing them into an industrial brotherhood, each part of which can at least understand of the others that they are working for one great and common end. This bond of unionism is stronger than one can read-ily imagine who has not seen its mysterious workings or who has not been a victim of its members' newly found enthusiasm. It is to-day the strongest tie that can bind together 147,000 mine workers and the thousands dependent upon them. It is more than religion, more

2. "The Slav Invasion," by F. J. Warne, pages 118, 119.

than the social ties which hold together members of the same community."

It was during a remarkable struggle on the part of this amalgamation of men from all countries, that the United States government, in spite of itself, was driven to take a hand in an industrial situation, owing to the long strain and the intolerable suffering entailed upon the whole country. Even then, however, the Government endeavored to confine its investigation to the mere commercial questions of tonnage and freight rates with their political implications, and it was only when an aroused and moralized public opinion insisted upon it that the national commission was driven to consider the human aspects of the case. Because of this public opinion, columns of newspapers and days of investigation were given to the discussion of the deeds of violence, discussions having nothing to do with the original demands of the strikers and entering only into the value set upon human life by each of the contesting parties. Did the union encourage violence against non-union men, or did it really do everything to suppress violence? Did it live up to its creed which was to maintain a standard of living that families might be properly housed and protected from debilitating toil and disease, and that children might be nurtured into American citizenship? Did the operators protect their men as far as possible from mine damp, from length of hours proven by experience to be exhausting? Did they pay a wage to the mine laborer sufficient to allow him to send his children to school? Questions such as these, a study of the human problem, invaded the commission day after day during the sitting. One felt for the moment the first wave of a rising tide of humanitarianism, until the normal ideals of the laborer to secure food and shelter for his family, a security for his own old age, and a larger opportunity for his children became the ideals of democratic government.

Let us imagine the result if, during the long anthracite strike, the humane instinct had so over-mastered the minds of the strikers, and so exalted their passions that they had lifted a hand against no man, even though he seemed to be endangering their cause before their eyes. Such a result might have come about, partly because the destruction of life had become abhorrent and impossible to them engaged as they were in the endeavor to raise life in the coal regions to a higher level, and partly because they would have scorned to destroy an enemy in order to achieve a mere negative result when the power lay within themselves to convert him into an ally, when they might have made him a source of help and power, a comrade of the same undertaking. If the element of battle, of mere self-seeking, could be eliminated from strikes, if they could remain a sheer uprising of the oppressed and underpaid to a self-conscious recognition of their condition, so unified, so irresistible as to sweep all the needy within its flood, we should have a tide rising, not to destruction, but to beneficence. Let us imagine the state of public feeling if there had been absolutely no act of violence traceable, directly or indirectly, to the union miners; if during the long months of the strike the great body of miners could have added the sanction of sustained conduct to their creed. Public sympathy would have led to an understanding of the need these miners were trying to meet, and the American nation itself might have been ready to ask for legislation concerning the minimum wage, and for protection to life and limb, equal to the legislation of New Zealand or Germany. But because the element of warfare unhappily did exist, government got back to its old business of repression.

To preserve law and order is obviously the function of government everywhere; and yet in our complicated modern society, especially as thousands of varied peoples are crowded into cities, it is not always easy to see just where real social order lies. The officials themselves are sometimes perplexed, and at other times deliberately use the devices of government for their own ends. We may take once more in illustration the great strike in the Chicago stock-yards. The immediate object of the strike was the protection of the wages of the unskilled men from a cut of one cent per hour, although, of course, the unions of skilled men felt that this first invasion of the wages increased through the efforts of the union, would be but the entering wedge of an attempt to cut wages in all the trades represented in the stock-yards. Owing to the refusal on the part of the unions to accept arbitration offered by the packers at an embarrassing moment, and because of the failure of the unions to carry out the terms of a contract, the strike in its early stages completely lost the sympathy of that large part of the public dominated by ideals of business honor and fair dealing. It lost, too, the sympathy of that growing body of organized labor which is steadily advancing in a regard for the validity of the contract, and is faithfully cherishing the hope that in time the trades unions may universally attain an accredited business standing.

The leaders after the first ten days were, therefore, forced to make the most of the purely human appeal which lay in the situation itself, that 30,000 men, including the allied trades, were losing weeks of wages, with a possible chance of the destruction of their unions on behalf of the unskilled who were the newly arrived Poles and Lithuanians, unable as yet to look out for themselves. Owing to the irregular and limited hours of work—a condition quite like that prevailing on the London docks before the great strike of the dockers—the weekly wage of these unskilled men was exceptionally low, and the plea of the strikers was based upon the duty of the strong to the weak. A chivalric call was issued that the standard of life might be raised to that designated as American, and that this mass of unskilled men might secure an education for their children. Of course no appeal could have been so strong as this purely human one which united for weeks thousands of men of a score of nationalities into that solidarity which only comes through a self-sacrificing devotion to an absorbing cause.

The strike involved much suffering and many unforeseen complications. At the end of eight weeks the union leaders made the best terms possible. Through these terms the skilled workers were guaranteed against a reduction in wages, but no provision was made for the unskilled in whose behalf the strike had at first been undertaken. Although the hard-pressed leaders were willing to make this concession, the politicians in the meanwhile had seen the great value of the human sentiment which bases its appeal on the need of the under dog and which had successfully united this mass of workingmen into a new comradeship with the immigrants. The appeal was infinitely more valuable than any merely political cry, and the fact that the final terms of settlement were submitted to a referendum vote at once gave the local politicians a chance to avail themselves of this big, loosely defined sympathy. They did avail themselves of this in so dramatic a manner that they almost succeeded, solely upon that appeal, in taking the strike out of the hands of the legitimate officers and placing it in their own hands for their own political ends.

The situation was a typical one, exemplifying the real aim of popular government with its concern for primitive needs, forced to seek expression outside of the organized channels of government. If the militia could have been called in, government would have been placed even more dramatically in the position of the oppressor of popular self-government. The phenomenal good order, the comparative lack of violence on the part of the striking workmen, gave no chance for the bringing in of the militia. The city politician was of course very much disappointed, for it would have afforded him an opening to put the odium of this traditional opposition of government, an opposition which has always been most dramatically embodied in the soldier, upon the political party dominating the State but not the city. It would have given the city politician an excellent opportunity to show the concern of himself and his party for the real people, as over against the attitude of the party dominating the State. But because the militia was not called, his scheme failed, and the legitimate strike leaders who, although they passed through much tribulation because of this political interference, did not eventually lose control.

The situation in the Chicago stock-yards also afforded an excellent epitome of the fact that government so often finds itself, not only in opposition to the expressed will of the people making the demand at the moment, but apparently against the best instincts of the mass of the citizens as a whole.

For years the city administration had so protected the property interests invested in the stockyards, that none of the sanitary ordinances had ever been properly enforced. The sickening stench and the scum on the branch of the river known as Bubbly Creek at times made that section of the city unendurable. The smoke ordinances were openly ignored, nor did the meat inspector ever seriously interfere with business, being quite willing to have meat sold in Chicago which had not passed the inspection for foreign markets. The water steals, too, for which the stock-yards were at one time notorious, must have been more or less known to certain officials. But all this merely corrupted a limited number of inspectors, and although their corruption was complete and involved entire administrations, it did not actually touch large numbers of persons. During the strike of 1904, however, 1,200 policemen, actual men possessed of human sensibilities, were called upon to patrol the yards inside and out. There is no doubt that the police inspector of the district thoroughly represented the alliance of the City Hall with the business interests, that he did not mean to discover anything which was derogatory to the packers nor to embarrass them in any way during the conduct of the strike. Had these 1,200 men, more than a regiment in numbers, been a regiment in training and tradition, they, too, would have seen nothing, and would have been content at heart, as they were obliged to be in conduct, to have arrested the strikers on the slightest provocation, and to have protected the strike-breakers.

But they were, in point of fact, called upon to face a very peculiar situation, because of the type of men and women who formed the bulk of the strike-breakers, and because, during the first weeks of the strike, these men and women were kept constantly inside the yards, day and night. In order to hold them at all, discipline outside of working hours was thoroughly relaxed, and the policemen in charge of the yards, while there ostensibly to enforce law and order, were obliged every night to connive at prize-fighting, at open gambling, and at prostitution. They were there, not to enforce law and order as it defines itself in the minds of the bulk of healthy-minded citizens, but only to keep the strikers from molesting the non-union workers. This was certainly commendable, but, after all, only part of their real duty.

Because they were normal men living in the midst of normal life and not in barracks, they were shocked by the law-breaking which they were ordered to protect, and much drawn in sympathy to the strikers whom they were supposed to regard as public enemies. An investigator who interviewed one hundred policemen found only one who did not frankly extol the virtues of the strikers as over against the shocking vices of the imported men. This, of course, was an extreme case brought about by the unusual and peculiar type of the imported strike-breakers. There is, however, trustworthy evidence incorporated in affidavits which were at the time submitted to the Mayor of Chicago, concerning the unlawful conduct of the men who were under the protection of the city police.

It was hard for a patriot not to feel jealous of the union and of the enthusiasm of those newly emigrated citizens. They poured out their gratitude and affection upon this first big friendly force which had offered them help in their desperate struggle in the New World. This devotion, this comradeship, and this fine *esprit de corps* should have been won by the Government itself from these newly arrived, scared, and untrained citizens. The union was that which had concerned itself with the real struggle for life, shelter, a chance to work, and bread for their children. It had come to them in a language they could understand, through men with interests akin to their own, and it gave them both their first chance to express themselves through a democratic vote, and an opportunity to register by a ballot their real opinion upon a very important matter.

They used the referendum votes, the latest and perhaps the most clever device of democratic government, and yet they used it to decide a question which the government supposed to be quite outside its realm. When they left the old country, the government of America held their deepest hopes, and represented that which they believed would obtain for them the fullness of life denied them in the lands of oppressive governments. It is a curious commentary on the fact that we have not yet attained self-government when the real and legitimate objects of men's desires must still be incorporated in those voluntary groups for which the government, when it does its best, can only afford protection from interference. As the religious revivalist looks with longing upon the fervor of a single-tax meeting, as the orthodox Jew sees his son stay away from Yom Kippur service in order to pour all his religious fervor, his precious zeal for righteousness which has been gathered through the centuries, into the Socialist Labor Party—so a patriot finds himself exclaiming to the immigrant, like another Andrea del Sarto to his wife, "Oh, but what do they—what do they to please you more?"

The stock-yards strike afforded an example of the national appeal subordinated to an appeal made in the name of labor. During the early stages of the strike it was discovered that newly arrived Macedonians were taking many of the places vacated by the strikers. One of the most touching scenes during the strike was the groups of Macedonians who would sit together in the twilight playing on primitive pipes singularly like the one which is associated with the great god Pan. The slender song would carry amazingly in the smoke-bedimmed air, affecting the spectator with a curious sense of incongruity.

When the organized labor of Chicago discovered that the strikers' places were taken by Greeks, the unions threatened, unless the Greeks were "called off," to boycott the Greek fruit-dealers all over the city, who with their street stands are singularly dependent upon the patronage of workingmen. The fact that the strike-breakers were Macedonians, as it happened, was an additional advantage at the moment; for the Greeks have been much concerned to make it clear that Macedonia belongs to Greece, and have hotly resented the efforts of Bulgaria to establish a protectorate over the country. They therefore responded at once to this acknowledgment of their claim, and, partly to show that the Macedonians and Greeks were countrymen, partly because they resented the implication that a Greek could act a cowardly part in any situation, and also, doubtless, because they were merchants threatened with loss of trade, they made superhuman efforts to clear the yards of Macedonians. This they accomplished in a remarkably short time. So reckless were they in the methods they used that it was common gossip throughout the Greek colony that strike-breakers would be refused the comforts of religion by the Greek priests in the city, although doubtless this rumor was unfounded. This utter recklessness of method, this determination to deter strike-breaking at any cost, is, of course, a revelation of the war element which is an essential part of any strike. The appeal to "loyalty" is the nearest approach to a moral appeal which can be safely made in the midst of a war of any sort. During a long strike one result of the non-moral appeal is to confuse the situation so that it becomes utterly impossible to tell how many men refuse to become strike-breakers because they are terrorized and how many stay away from conviction. The non-moral appeal not only sins against the principles advocated by trades unionists, but it contradicts itself and brings great confusion into the situation, as war ideals always do when thrust into a peaceful society. It was, for instance, quite impossible to tell whether the lowering in the type of man who was willing to take a striker's place, so that at last only very ignorant men from the southern plantations could be induced to work, was due to a species of class consciousness, a response to the demand felt so strongly by labor men—"Thou shalt not take thy neighbor's job"—or whether workingmen are becoming so afraid to take striker's places that these places must at last be given to men who have come from such remote parts of the country that "they do not know enough to be afraid." The unions themselves could take no accounting of their real strength because of the terrorism which had become thrust into the situation. And yet all that the stock-yards workers were demanding through this long and disastrous strike, was the minimum wage which has been guaranteed by conservative governments elsewhere, and is recognized even in the United States in much governmental work under the contracts of civil or Federal authorities. So timid are American cities, however, in dealing with this perfectly reasonable subject of wages in its relation to municipal employees, that when they do prescribe a minimum wage for city contract work, they allow it to fall into the hands of the petty politician and to become part of a political game, making no effort to give it a dignified treatment in relation to the cost of living and to the margin of leisure. In this the English cities have anticipated us, both as to time and legitimate procedure. Have Americans formed a sort of "imperialism of virtue," holding on to preconceived ideals of government and insisting that they must fit all the people who come to our shores, even though they crush the most promising bits of self-expression in the process? Is the American attitude toward self-government like that of the Anglo-Saxon towards civilization, save that he goes forth to rule all the nations of the earth by one pattern, while we remain at home and bid them to rule themselves by one pattern? We firmly decline not only to consider matters of industry and commerce as germane to government, but we also decline to bring men together upon that most natural and inevitable of all foundations, their industrial needs.

The government which refuses to consider matters of this sort, or at least waits until their neglect becomes a scandal before it consents to deal with them, as a result of this caution forces the most patriotic citizens to ignore the Government and to embody their scruples and hopes of progress in voluntary organizations. To be afraid to extend the functions of government may be to lose what we have. A government has always received feeble support from its constituents as soon as its demands appeared childish or remote. Citizens inevitably neglect or abandon civic duty, when their government no longer embodies their genuine desires. It is useless to hypnotize ourselves by unreal talk of colonial ideas, and of our patriotic duty towards immigrants as though the situation was one demanding the passage of a set of resolutions when we fail to realize that the nation can be saved only by patriots who are possessed of a contemporaneous knowledge.

As industrial relations imply peaceful relations, under a certain rough reorganization and reconstruction of governmental functions which the association of labor presents, it is inevitable that in its international aspects the association should formally advocate universal peace. Workmen have always realized, however feebly and vaguely they may have expressed it, that it is they who in all ages have borne the heaviest burden of privation and suffering imposed on the world by the military spirit.

The first international organization founded, not to promote a colorless peace, but to advance and develop the common life of all nations, was founded in London in 1864 by workingmen, and was called simply "The International Association of Workingmen." They recognized that a supreme interest raised all workingmen above the prejudice of race, and united them by wider and deeper principles than those by which they were separated into nations. They hoped that as religion, science, art, had become international, so now at last labor might take its place as an international interest. A few years later, at its third congress in Brussels they recommended that in case of war a universal strike be declared.

There is a growing conviction among workingmen of all countries that, whatever may be accomplished by a national war, however moral the supposed aim of such a war, there is one inevitable result—an increased standing army, the soldiers of which are non-producers, and must be fed by the workers.

The surprising growth of Socialism, at the moment, is due largely to the fact that it is the only political party upon an international basis, and also that it frankly ventures its future upon a better industrial organization. These two aspects have had much more to do with its hold in industrial neighborhoods than have its philosophic tenets or the impassioned appeal of its propagandists. The Socialists are making almost the sole attempt to preach a morality sufficiently all-embracing and international to keep pace with even that material internationalism which has standarized the threads of screws and the size of bolts, so that machines may become interchangeable from one country to another. It is the same sort of internationalism which Mazzini preached when distracted Italy was making her desperate struggle for a unified and national life. He issued his remarkable address to her workingmen and solemnly told them that the life of the nation could not be made secure until her patriots were ready to die for human issues. He saw, earlier than most men, that the desire to be at unity with all human beings, to claim the sense of a universal affection is a force not to be ignored. He believed that it might even then be strong enough to devour the flimsy stuff called national honor, glory, and prestige, which incite to war and induce workingmen to trample over each other's fields and to destroy the results of each other's labor.

Workingmen dream of an industrialism which shall be the hand-maid of a commerce ministering to an increased power of consumption among the producers of the world, binding them together in a genuine internationalism. Existing commerce has long ago reached its international stage, but it has been the result of business aggression and constantly appeals for military defense and for the forcing of new markets. In so far as commerce has rested upon the successful capture of the resources of the workers, it has been a relic of the mediaeval baron issuing forth to seize the merchants' boats as they passed his castle on the Rhine. It has logically lent itself to warfare, and is, indeed, the modern representative of conquest. As its prototype rested upon slavery and vassalage, so this commerce is founded upon a contempt for the worker and believes that he can live on low wages. It assumes that his legitimate wants are the animal ones comprising merely food and shelter and the cost of replacement. The industrialism of which this commerce is a part, exhibits this same contemptuous attitude, but it is more easily extended to immigrants than to any other sort of work-men because they seem further away from a common standard of life. This attitude toward the immigrant simply illustrates once more that it is around the deeply significant idea of the standard of life that our industrial problems of to-day centre. The desire for a higher standard of living in reality forms the base of all the forward movements of the working class. "The significance of the standard of life lies not so much in the fact that for each of us it is different, as that for all of us it is pro-gressive,"[3] constantly invading new realms. To imagine that for immi-grants it is merely a question of tin cups and plates stored in a bunk *versus* a white cloth and a cottage table, and that all goes well if sewing-machines and cottage-organs reach the first generation of immigrants,

3. *The Standard of Life*, by Mrs. Bernard Bosenquet, page 4.

and fashionable dressmakers and pianos the second, is of course a most untutored interpretation. Until the standard of life is apprehended in its real significance and made the crux of the immigrant situation, as recent economists are making the power of consumption the test of a nation's prosperity, we shall continue to ignore the most obvious and natural basis for understanding and mutual citizenship.

Because workmen have been forced to consider this standard of living in regard to immigrants as well as themselves, they have made genuine efforts toward amalgamation. This is perhaps easily explained, for, after all, the man in this country who realizes human equality is not he who repeats the formula of the eighteenth century, but he who has learned that the "idea of equality is an outgrowth of man's primary relations with nature. Birth, growth, nutrition, reproduction, death, are the great levelers that remind us of the essential equality of human life. It is with the guarantee of equal opportunities to play our parts well in these primary processes that government is chiefly concerned"[4] and not merely with the repression of the vicious, nor with guarding the rights of property. All that devotion of the trades union for the real issues and trials of life could, of course, easily be turned into a passion for self-government and for the development of the national life if we were really democratic from the modern evolutionary standpoint, and held our town-meetings upon the topics of vital concern.

So long, however, as the Government declines to concern itself with these deeper issues involved in the standard of life and the industrial status of thousands of its citizens, we must lose it.

If progress were inaugurated by those members of the community who possess the widest knowledge and superior moral insight, then social amelioration might be brought about without the bungling and mistakes which so distress us all. But, over and over again, salutary changes are projected and carried through by men of even less than the average ethical development, because their positions in life have brought them in contact with the ills of existing arrangements. To quote from John Morley: "In matters of social improvement, the most common reason why one hits upon a point of progress and not another, is that one happens to be more directly touched than the other by the

4. *The American City,* Delos F. Wilcox, page 200.

unimproved practice."[5] Perhaps this is a sufficient explanation of the fact that untrained workmen are entrusted with the difficult task of industrial amelioration and adjustment, while the rest of the community often seems ignorant of the truth that institutions which do not march with the extension of human needs and relationships are dead, and may easily become a deterrent to social progress. Unless we subordinate class interests and class feeling to a broader conception of social progress, unless we take pains to come in contact with the surging and diverse peoples who make up the nation, we cannot hope to attain a sane social development. We need rigid enforcement of the existing laws, while at the same time, we frankly admit the inadequacy of these laws, and work without stint for progressive regulations better fitted to the newer issues among which our lot is cast; for, unless the growing conscience is successfully embodied in legal enactment, men lose the habit of turning to the law for guidance and redress.

I recall, in illustration of this, an instance which took place fifteen years ago. I had newly come to Chicago, fresh from the country, and had little idea of the social and industrial conditions in which I found myself on Halsted Street, when a dozen girls came from a neighboring factory with a grievance in regard to their wages. The affair could hardly have been called a labor difficulty. The girls had never heard of a trades union, and were totally unaccustomed to acting together. It was more in the nature of a "scrap" between themselves and their foreman. In the effort toward adjustment, there remains vividly in my memory a conversation I had with a leading judge who arbitrated the difficulty. He expressed his belief in the capacity of the common law to meet all legitimate labor difficulties as they arise. He trusted its remarkable adaptabiilty to changing conditions under the decisions of wise and progressive judges. He contended, however, that, in order to adjust it to our industrial affairs, it must be interpreted, not so much in relation to precedents established under a judicial order which belongs to the past, but in reference to that newer sense of justice which this generation is seeking to embody in industrial relations. He foresaw something of the stress and storm of the industrial conflicts which have occurred in Chicago since then, and he expressed the hope that the Bench of Cook

5. *Compromise,* John Morley, page 213.

County might seize the opportunity, in this new and difficult situation, of dealing with labor difficulties in a judicial spirit.

What a difference it would have made in the history of Chicago during the last fifteen years if more men had been possessed of this temper and wisdom, and had refused to countenance the use of force. If more men had been able to see the situation through a fresher medium; to apprehend that the old legal enactments were too individualistic and narrow; that a difference in degree may make a difference in kind; if they had realized that they were the first generation of American jurists who had to deal with a situation made novel by the fact that it was brought about by the coming together of two millions of people largely on an industrial basis!

Our constitutions were constructed by the advanced men of the eighteenth century, who had studied the works of the most radical thinkers of that century. Radicalism then meant a more democratic political organization, and in its defence, they fearlessly quoted the Greek city and the Roman Forum. But we have come to admit that our present difficulties are connected with our industrial organization and with the lack of connection between that organization and our inherited democratic form of government. If self-government were to be inaugurated by the advanced men of the present moment, they would make a most careful research into those early organizations of village communities, folk-motes, and mirs, those primary cells of both industrial and political organizations, where the people knew no difference between the two, but, quite simply, met to consider in common discussion all that concerned their common life. They would investigate the crafts, guilds, and artels, which combine government with daily occupations, as did the self-governing university and free town. They would seek for the connection between the liberty-loving mediaeval city and its free creative architecture, that art which combines the greatest variety of artists and artisans. They would not altogether ignore the "compulsion of origins" and the fact that our present civilization is most emphatically an industrial one. In Germany, when the Social Democratic party first vigorously asserted the economic basis of society and laid the emphasis upon its industrial aspect, the Government itself, in a series of legislative measures, designated "the Socialism of Bismarck," found itself dealing directly with industry, through a sheer effort to give itself a touch of reality. The Government of Russia, in the first year of the Japanese War, made an effort to relieve the needs of the people. The bureaucracy itself organized the workmen into a species of trades unions through which the Russian Government promised to protect the proletarian from the aggressions of capital. The entire incident was suggestive of the protection afforded by the central State to the slowly emancipated serfs of central Europe when the barons, reluctant to give up their rights and privileges, so unjustly oppressed them.

Shall a democracy be slower than these old Powers to protect its humblest citizen, and shall it see them slowly deteriorating because, according to democratic theory, they do not need protection?

V

Group Morality in the
Labor Movement

This generation is constantly confronted by radical industrial changes, from which the community as a whole profits, but which must inevitably bring difficulty of adjustment and disaster to men of certain trades. In all fairness, these difficulties should be distributed and should not be allowed to fall completely upon the group of working-people whose labor is displaced as a result of the changes and who are obliged to learn anew their method of work and mode of life.

If the great industrial changes could be considered as belonging to the community as a whole and could be reasonably dealt with, the situation would then be difficult enough, but it is enormously complicated by the fact that society has become divided into camps in relation to the industrial system and that many times the factions break out into active hostility. These two camps inevitably develop group morality—the employers tending toward the legal and contractual development of morality, the workingmen toward the sympathetic and human. Among our contemporaries, these two are typified by the employers associations and the trades unions.

It is always difficult to judge a contemporaneous movement with any degree of fairness, and it is perennially perplexing to distinguish what is merely adventitious and temporary from that which represents essential and permanent tendencies. This discrimination is made much more difficult when a movement exhibits various stages of development contemporaneously, then a dozen historic phases are going on at the same time. Yet every historic movement towards democracy, which constantly gathers to itself large bodies of raw recruits while the older groups are moving on, presents this peculiar difficulty. In the case of trades unions, certain groups are marked by lawlessness and disorder, others by most decorous business methods, and still others are fairly decadent in their desire for monopolistic control. It is a long cry from the Chartists of 1839, burning hayricks, to John Burns of 1902, pleading in the House of Commons with well-reasoned eloquence for an extension of the workingmen's franchise. Nevertheless they are both manifestations of the same movement towards universal suffrage and show no greater difference than that between the Chicago teamsters, who were blocking commerce and almost barricading the streets in 1902 when at the same moment John Mitchell made his well-considered statement that he would rather lose the coal strike, with all that that loss implied, than gain it at the cost of violence. Students of industrial history will point out the sequence and development of the political movement from the Chartist to the Independent Labor party. They will tell us that the same desire burned in the hearts of the ignorant farmers which fired the distinguished parliamentarian, but they give no help to our bewildered minds when we would fain discover some order and sequence between the widely separated events of the contemporaneous labor movement.

We must first get down to the question, In what does "the inevitably destined rise of the men of labor" consist? What are we trying to solve in this "most hazardous problem of the age"? Is progress in the labor movement to come, as we are told progress comes in the non-moral world, by the blind, brute struggle of individual interests; or is it to come, as its earlier leaders believed, through the operation of the human will? Is it a question of morals which must depend upon educators and apostles; or is it merely a conflict of opposing rights which may legitimately use coercion? The question, from the very nature of the case, is confusing; for, of necessity, the labor movement has perfectly legitimate economic and business aspects, which loom large and easily overshadow the ethical. We would all agree that only when men have education, a margin of leisure, and a decent home can they find room to develop the moral life. Before that, there are too many chances that it will be crushed out by ignorance, by grinding weariness, and by indecency. But the danger lies in the conviction that these advantages are to be secured by any means, moral or non-moral, and in holding them paramount to the inner life which they are supposed to nourish. The labor movement is confronted by that inevitable problem which confronts every movement and every individual. How far shall the compromise be made between the inner concept and the outer act? How may we concede what it is necessary to concede, without conceding all?

We constantly forget that, in the last analysis, the spiritual growth of one social group is conditioned by the reaction of other social groups upon it. We ignore the fact that the worship of success, so long dominant in America, has taught the majority of our citizens to count only accomplishment and to make little inquiry concerning methods. Success has become the sole standard in regard to business enterprises and political parties, but it is evident that the public intends to call a halt before it is willing to apply the same standard to labor organizations.

It is clear that the present moment is one of unusual crisis—that many of the trades unions of America have reached a transitional period, when they can no longer be mere propagandists, but are called upon to deal with concrete and difficult situations. When they were small and persecuted, they held to the faith and its implication of idealism. As they become larger and more powerful, they make terms with the life about them, and compromise as best they may with actual conditions.

The older unions, which have reached the second stage that may be described as that of business dealing, are constantly hampered and harassed by the actions of the younger unions which are still in the enthusiastic stage. This embarrassment is especially notable just now, for, during this last period of prosperity, trades unions have increased enormously in numbers; the State Federation of Minnesota, for instance, reported an increase of six hundred per cent. in one year. Nearly all the well-established unions have been flooded by new members who are not yet assimilated and disciplined.

During this period of extraordinary growth, the labor movement has naturally attracted to itself hundreds of organizations which are yet in their infancy and exhibit all the weakness of "group morality." This doubtless tends to a conception of moral life which is as primitive as that which controlled the beginnings of patriotism, when the members of the newly conscious nation considered all those who were outside as possible oppressors and enemies, and were loyal only towards those whom their imagination included as belonging to the national life. They gave much, and demanded much, in the name of blood brothers, but were merciless to the rest of the world. In addition to its belligerent youth and its primitive morality, the newer union is prone to declare a strike, simply because the members have long suffered what they consider to be grievances, and the accumulated sense of unredressed wrong makes them eager for a chance to "fight for their rights." At the same time, the employer always attempts his most vigorous attack upon a new union, both because he does not wish organized labor to obtain a foothold in his factory, and because his chances for success are greater before his employees are well disciplined in unionism. Nevertheless in actual conflict a young union will often make a more reckless fight than an older one, like the rough rider in contrast with the disciplined soldier. The members of a newly organized group naturally respond first to a sense of loyalty to each other as against their employers, and then to the wider consciousness of organized labor as against capital. This stage of trades unionism is full of war phraseology, with its "pickets" and "battle-grounds," and is responsible for the most serious mistakes of the movement.

The sense of group loyalty holds trades unionists longer than is normal to other groups, doubtless because of the constant accessions of those who are newly conscious of its claims.

Those Chicago strikes, which, during the last few years, have been most notably characterized by disorder and the necessity for police interference, have almost universally been inaugurated by the newly organized unions. They have called to their aid the older organizations, and the latter have entered into the struggle many times under protest and most obviously against their best interests.

The Chicago Federation of Labor has often given its official indorsement to hot-headed strikes on the part of "baby unions" because the delegates from the newly organized or freshly recruited unions had the larger vote, and the appeal to loyalty and to fraternity carried the meeting against the judgment of the delegates from the older unions.

The members of newly organized unions more readily respond to the appeal to strike, in that it stirs memory of their "organization night," when they were admitted after solemn ceremonies into the American Federation of Labor. At the same time, the organizers themselves often hold out too large promises, on the sordid side, of what organization will be able to accomplish. They tell the newly initiated what other unions have done, without telling at the same time how long they have been organized and how steadily they have paid dues. Several years ago, when there seemed to be a veritable "strike fever" in Chicago among the younger trades unions, it was suggested in the Federation of Labor that no union be authorized to declare a strike until it had been organized for at least two years. The regulation was backed by some of the strongest and wisest trades unionists, but it failed to pass because the organizers were convinced that it would cripple them in forming new unions. They would be obliged to point to many months of patient payment of dues and humdrum meetings before any real gain could be secured. The organizers, in fact, are in the position of a recruiting officer who is obliged to tell his raw material of all the glories of war, but at the same time bid them remember that warfare is always inexpedient. He must advise them to take a long and tedious training in the arts of diplomacy and in the most advanced methods of averting war before any action can possibly be considered.

In point of fact the organizers do not do this, and many men join unions expecting that a strike will be speedily declared which will settle all the difficulties of modern industrialism. It is, therefore, not so remarkable that strikes should occur often and should exhibit warlike features. What is remarkable is the attitude of the public which has certainly eliminated the tactics of war in other civil relations.

A tacit admission that a strike is war and that all the methods of warfare are permissible was made in Chicago during the teamsters' strike of 1905, when there was little protest against the war method of conducting a struggle between two private organizations, one of employer and one of employed. Why should the principles of legal adjustment have been thus complacently flung to the winds by the two millions of citizens who had no direct interest in this struggle, but whose pursuits in business were interfered with, whose safety on the streets was imperiled, and whose moral sensibilities were outraged?

How did the public become hypnotized into a passive endurance of a street warfare in which two associations were engaged, like feudal chiefs with their recalcitrant retainers? In those similar cases, when blood grew too hot on both sides, the mediaeval emperor intervened and compelled peace. General public opinion is our hard-won substitute for the emperor's personal will. Public opinion, however, did not assert itself and interfere—on the contrary, the entire town acquiesced in the statement of the contestants that this method of warfare was the only one possible, and thereupon yielded to a tendency to overvalue physical force and to ignore the subtler and less obvious conditions on which the public welfare rests. At that time all methods of arbitration and legal redress were completely set aside.

There is no doubt but that ideas and words which at one time fill a community with enthusiasm may, after a few years, cease to be a moving force, apparently from no other reason than that they are spent and no longer fit into the temper of the hour. Such a fate has evidently befallen the word "arbitration," at least in Chicago, as it is applied to industrial struggles. Almost immediately following the labor disturbances of 1894 in Chicago, the agitation was begun for a State Board of Arbitration, resulting in legislation and the appointment of the Illinois Board. At that time the public believed that arbitration would go far towards securing industrial peace, or at least that it would provide the device through which labor troubles could be speedily adjusted, and during that period there was much talk concerning compulsory arbitration with reference to the successful attempts in New Zealand.

During the industrial struggles of later years, however, not only are the services of the State Board rejected, but voluntary bodies constantly find their efforts less satisfactory. Employers contend that arbitration implies the yielding of points on both sides. Since, however, most boards of arbitration provide that grievances must be submitted to them before the strike occurs, and the men are thus kept at work while the grievances are being considered, the men therefore have virtually nothing to lose by declaring a strike. They are subjected to a temptation to constantly formulate new demands, because, without losing time or pay, they are almost certain to secure some concession, however small, in their favor. The employers in the teamsters' strike thus explained their position when they declared that there was nothing which could be submitted to arbitration. These employers also contended that the ordinary court has no precedent for dealing with questions of hours and wages, of shop rules, and many other causes of trade-union disputes, because all these matters are new as questions of law and can be satisfactorily adjusted only through industrial courts in which tradition and precedent bearing upon modern industrial conditions have been accumulated. The rise and fall of wages affect not one firm only, but a national industry, and even the currents of international trade, so that it is impossible to treat of them as matters in equity. With this explanation, the Chicago public rested content during the long weeks of the teamsters' strike, for no one pointed out that these arguments did not apply to this particular situation, so accustomed have we grown in Chicago to warfare as a method of settling labor disputes. The charges of the Employers' Association against the teamsters did not involve any points demanding adjustment through industrial courts. The charges the Employers' Association made were those of broken contracts, of blackmail, and of conspiracy, all of them points which are constantly adjudicated in Cook County courts.

It was constantly asserted that officers of the Teamsters' Union demanded money from employers in the height of the busy season in order to avert threatened strikes; that there was a disgraceful alliance between certain members of the Team Owners' Association and officers of the Teamsters' Union.

It would, of course, have been impossible to prove blackmail and the charges of "graft," unless the employers themselves or their representatives had borne testimony, which would inevitably have implicated themselves. During the first weeks of the strike, these charges were freely made, definite sums were named, and dates were given. There was also an offer on the part of various managers to make affidavits, but later they shrank from the publicity, and refused to give them, preferring apparently to throw the whole town into disorder rather than to "stand up" to the consequences of their own acts and to acknowledge the bribery to which they claim they were forced to resort. They demonstrated once more that a show of manliness and an appeal to arms may many times hide cowardice.

To throw affairs into a state of warfare is to put them where the moral aspect will not be scrutinized and where the mere interest of the game and a desire to watch it will be paramount.

The vicious combination represented by certain men in the Team Owners' Association and in the Teamsters' Union, "the labor and capital hunting together" kind, is a public menace which can be abolished only by a combined effort on the part of the best employers and the best labor men. The "better element" certainly were in a majority, for the most dangerous members of this sinister combination were at last reduced to fifteen or twenty men. These very men, however, after a prolonged strike, became either victors or martyrs, and in either case were firmly established in power and influence for the succeeding two years. Why should an entire city of two million people have been put to such an amazing amount of inconvenience and financial loss, with their characters brutalized as well, in order to accomplish this? The traditional burning of the house in order to roast the pig is quite outdone by this overturning of a city in order to catch a "score of rascals," for in the end the rascals are not caught, and it is as if the house were burned and the pig had escaped. Was it not the result of acting under military fervor? Over and over again it has been found that organizations based upon a mutual sense of grievance or of outrage have always been militant, for while men cannot be formed permanently into associations whose chief bond is a sense of exasperation and wrong dealing, during the time they are thus held together they are committed to aggressive action.

Moral rights and duties formed upon the relations of man to man are applicable to all situations, and to deny this applicability to a difficult case, is to beg the entire question. The consequences do not stop there, for we all know that to deny the validity of the moral principle in one relation is to sap its strength in all relations.

Employers often resent being obliged to have business relations with workingmen, although they no longer say that they will refuse to deal with them, as a woman still permits herself to say that she "will not argue with a servant." They nevertheless contend that the men are unreasonable, and that because it is impossible to establish contractual relations with them, they must be coerced. This contention goes far toward legitimatizing terrorism. It therefore seems to them defensible to refuse to go into the courts and to insist upon war because they do it from a consciousness of rectitude, although this insensibly slips into a consciousness of power, as self-righteousness is so prone to do. But these are all the traits of militant youth, which in the teamsters' strike was indeed borne out by the facts in the case.

The Employers' Association of Chicago was largely composed of merchants whose experience with trades unionism was almost limited to the Teamsters' Union which has been in existence for only five years and, from the first, has been truculent and difficult. Had the employers involved been manufacturers instead of merchants, they would have had years of experience with unions of skilled men, and they would have more nearly learned to adjust their personal and business relations to trades unionism. When an entire class in a community confess that without an appeal to arms they cannot deal with trades unions, who, after all, represent a national and international movement a hundred years old, they practically admit that they cannot manage their business under the existing conditions of modern life. To a very great extent it is a confession of weakness, to a very great extent a confession of frailty of temper. To make the adjustment to the peculiar problems of one's own surroundings is the crux of life's difficulties. "New organizations" and "new experiments in living" would not arise if there were not a certain inadequateness in existing organizations and ways of living. The new organizations and experiments may not point to the right mode of meeting the situation, but they do point to the existence of inadequateness and the need of readjustment. Changes in business methods have been multiform during the past fifteen years, and Chicago business men who have made those other adjustments would certainly be able to deal with labor in its present organized form if they were not inhibited by certain concepts of their "group morality."

In the meantime the public, which has been powerless to interfere, can only point to the consequences of grave social import which are sure to result from a prolonged period of disturbance.

First, there is the sharp division of the community into classes, with its inevitable hostility and misunderstanding. Capital lines up on one side, and labor on the other, until the "fair-minded public" disappears and Chicago loses her democratic spirit which has always been her most precious possession. In its place is substituted loyalty to the side to which each man belongs, irrespective of the merits of the case—the "my country right or wrong" sentiment which we call patriotism only in war times, the blind adherence by which a man is attached against his will, as it were, to the blunders of "his own kind."

During the first week of the strike, I talked with labor men who were willing to admit that there were grounds for indictment against at least two of the officers in the teamsters' locals. During the third week of the strike all that was swept aside, and one heard only that the situation must be taken quite by itself, with no references to the first causes, that it was a strike of organized capital against organized labor, and that we could have no peace in Chicago until it was "fought to a finish."

Second, there is an enormous increase in the feeling of race animosity, beginning with the imported negro strike-breakers, and easily extending to "Dagoes" and all other distinct nationalities. The principle of racial and class equality is at the basis of American political life, and to wantonly destroy it is one of the gravest outrages against the Republic.

Chicago is preeminently a city of mixed nationalities. It is our problem to learn to live together in forbearance and understanding and to fuse all the nations of men into the newest and, perhaps, the highest type of citizenship. To accept this responsibility may constitute our finest contribution to the problems of American life, but we may also wantonly and easily throw away such an opportunity by the stirring up of race and national animosity which is so easily aroused and so reluctantly subsides.

Third, there is the spirit of materialism which controls the city and confirms the belief that, after all, brute force, a trial of physical strength, is all that counts and the only thing worthy of admiration. Any check on the moral consciousness is paralyzed when the belief is once established that success is its own justification. When the stream of this belief joins the current of class interest, the spirit of the prize fighters' ring which cheers the best round and worships the winner, becomes paramount. It is exactly that which appeals to the so-called "hoodlum," and his sudden appearance upon the street at such times and in such surprising numbers demonstrates that he realizes that he has come to his own. At the moment we all forget that the determination to sacrifice all higher considerations to business efficiency, to make the machine move smoothly at any cost, "to stick at nothing," may easily make a breach in the ethical constitution of society which can be made good only by years of painful reparation.

Fourth, there is the effect upon the children and the youth of the entire city, for the furrow of class prejudice, which is so easily run through a plastic mind, often leaves a life-long mark. Each morning during the long weeks of the strike, thousands of children at the more comfortable breakfast tables learned to regard labor unions as the inciters of riot and the instruments of evil, thousands of children at the less comfortable breakfast tables shared the impotent rage of their parents that "law is always on the side of capital," and both sets of children added to the horrors of Manchuria and Warsaw, which were then taking place, the pleasurable excitement that war had become domesticated upon their own streets. We may well believe that these impressions and emotions will be kept by these children as part of their equipment in life and that their moral conceptions will permanently tend toward group moralities and will be cast into a coarser mold.

In illustration of this point I may, perhaps, cite my experience during the Spanish War.

For ten years I had lived in a neighborhood which is by no means criminal, and yet during October and November of 1898 we were startled by seven murders within a radius of ten blocks. A little investigation of details and motives, the accident of a personal acquaintance with two of the criminals, made it not in the least difficult to trace the murders back to the influence of the war. Simple people who read of carnage and bloodshed easily receive suggestions. Habits of self-control which have been but slowly and imperfectly acquired quickly break down when such a stress is put upon them.

Psychologists intimate that action is determined by the selection of the subject upon which the attention is habitually fixed. The newspapers, the theatrical posters, the street conversations for weeks, had to do with war and bloodshed. Day after day, the little children on the street played at war and at killing Spaniards. The humane instinct, which keeps in abeyance the tendency to cruelty, as well as the growing belief that the life of each human being, however hopeless or degraded, is still sacred, gives way, and the more primitive instinct asserts itself.

There is much the same social result during a strike, in addition to the fact that the effect of the prolonged warfare upon the labor movement itself is most disastrous. The unions at such times easily raise into power the unscrupulous "leader," so-called. In times of tumult, the aggressive man, the one who is of bellicose temper, and is reckless in his statements, is the one who becomes a leader. It is a vicious circle—the more warlike the times, the more reckless the leader who is demanded, and his reckless course prolongs the struggle. Such men make their appeal to loyalty for the union, to hatred and to contempt for the "non-union" man. Mutual hate towards a non-unionist may have in it the mere beginnings of fellowship, the protoplasm of tribal fealty, but no more. When it is carried over into civilized life it becomes a social deterrent and an actual menace to social relations.

In a sense it is fair to hold every institution responsible for the type of man whom it tends to bring to the front, and the type of organization which clings to war methods must, of course, consider it nobler to yield to force than to justice. The earlier struggle of democracy was for its recognition as a possible form of government and the struggle is now on to prove democracy an efficient form of government. So the earlier struggles of trades unions were for mere existence, and the struggle has now passed into one for a recognition of contractual relations and collective bargaining which will make trades unions an effective industrial instrument. It is much less justifiable of course in the later effort than it was in the earlier to carry on the methods of primitive warfare.

This new effort, however, from the very nature of things, is bringing another type of union man into office and is modifying the entire situation. The old-time agitator is no longer useful and a cooler man is needed for collective bargaining. At the same time the employers must put forth a more democratic and a more reasonable type of man if they would bear their side of this new bargaining, so that it has come about quite recently that the first attempts have been made in Chicago towards controlling in the interests of business itself this natural tendency of group morality.

It may offer another example of business and commerce, affording us a larger morality than that which the moralists themselves teach. Certain it is that the industrial problems engendered by the industrial revolutions of the last century, and flung upon this century for solution, can never be solved by class warfare nor yet by ignoring their existence in the optimism of ignorance.

America is only beginning to realize, and has not yet formulated, all the implications of the factory system and of the conditions of living which this well-established system imposes upon the workers. As we feel it closing down upon us, moments of restlessness and resentment seize us all. The protest against John Mitchell's statement[1] that the American workingman has recognized that he is destined to remain a workingman, is a case in point. In their attempt to formulate and correct various industrial ills, trades unions are often blamed for what is inherent in the factory system itself and for those evils which can be cured only through a modification of that system. For instance, factory workers in general have for years exhibited a tendency to regulate the output of each worker to a certain amount which they consider a fair day's work, although to many a worker such a restricted output may prove to be less than a fair day's work. The result is, of course, disastrous to the workers themselves as well as to the factory management, for it doubtless is quite as injurious to a man's nervous system to retard his natural pace as it is to unduly accelerate it. The real trouble, which this "limitation" is an awkward attempt to correct, is involved in the fact that the intricate subdivision of factory work, and the lack of understanding on the part of employees of the finished product, has made an unnatural situation, in which the worker has no normal interest in his work and no direct relation to it. In the various makeshifts on the part of the manufacturer to supply motives which shall take the place of the natural ones so obviously missing, many devices have been resorted to, such as "speeding up" machinery, "setting the pace," and substituting "piece work" for day work. The manufacturers may justly say that they have been driven to these various expedients, not only by the factory conditions, but by the natural laziness of men. Nevertheless reaction from such a course is inevitably an uncompromising attempt on the part of the workers to protect themselves from overexertion and to regulate the output. The worst cases I have ever known have occurred in unorganized shops and have been unregulated and unaided by any trades union. The "pace setter" in such a shop is often driven out and treated with the same animosity which the "scab" receives in a union shop.

In the same spirit we blame trades unionists for that disgraceful attitude which they have from time to time taken against the introduction of improved machinery—a small group blindly attempting to defend what they consider their only chance to work. The economists have

1. *Organized Labor,* John Mitchell, Preface.

done surprisingly little to shed light upon this difficulty; indeed, they are somewhat responsible for its exaggeration. Their old theory of a "wage fund" which did not reach the rank and file of trades unionists until at least in its first form it had been abandoned by the leading economists, has been responsible both for much disorder along this line, and for the other mistaken attempt "to make work for more men."

A society which made some effort to secure an equitable distribution of the leisure and increased ease which new inventions imply would remove the temptations as well as the odium of such action from the men who are blinded by what they consider an infringement of their rights.

If the wonderful inventions of machinery, as they came along during the last century, could have been regarded as in some sense social possessions, the worst evils attending the factory system of production—starvation wages, exhausting hours, unnecessary monotony, child labor, and all the rest of the wretched list—might have been avoided in the interest of society itself. All this would have come about had human welfare been earlier regarded as a legitimate object of social interest.

But no such ethics had been developed in the beginning of this century. Society regarded machinery as the absolute possession of the man who owned it at the moment it became a finished product, quite irrespective of the long line of inventors and workmen who represented its gradual growth and development. Society was, therefore, destined to all the maladjustment which this century has encountered. Is it the militant spirit once more as over against the newer humanitarianism? The possessor of the machine, like the possessor of arms who preceded him, regards it as a legitimate weapon for exploitation, as the former held his sword.

One of the exhibits in the Paris Exposition of 1900 presented a contrast between a mediaeval drawing of a castle towering above the hamlets of its protected serfs, and a modern photograph of the same hill covered with a huge factory which overlooked the villages of its dependent workmen. The two pictures of the same hill and of the same plain bore more than a geographic resemblance. This suggestion of modern exploitation would be impossible had we learned the first lessons which an enlarged industrialism might teach us. Class and group divisions with their divergent moralities become most dangerous when their members believe that the inferior group or class cannot be appealed to by reason and fair dealing, but must be treated upon a lower plane. Terrorism is considered necessary and legitimate that they may be inhibited by fear from committing certain acts. So far as employers exhibit this spirit toward workmen, or trades unionists toward non-unionists, they inevitably revert to the use of brute force—to the methods of warfare.

VI

Protection of Children for Industrial Efficiency

✍ In the previous chapters it was stated that the United States, compared to the most advanced European nations, is deficient in protective legislation. This, as has been said, is the result of the emphasis placed upon personal liberty at the date of the first constitutional conventions and of the inherited belief in America that government is of necessity oppressive, and its functions not to be lightly extended.

It is also possible that this protection of the humblest citizen has been pushed forward in those countries of a homogeneous population more rapidly than in America, because of that unconscious attitude of contempt which the nationality at the moment representing economic success always takes toward the weaker and less capable. There is no doubt that we all despise our immigrants a little because of their economic standing. The newly arrived immigrant goes very largely into unskilled work; he builds the railroads, digs the sewers, he does the sort of labor the English speaking American soon gets rid of; and then, because he is in this lowest economic class, he falls into need, and we complain that in America the immigrant makes the largest claim upon charitable funds. Yet in England, where immigration has counted for very little; in Germany, where it has counted almost not at all, we find the same claim made upon the public funds by people who do the same unskilled work, who are paid the same irregular and low wages. In Germany, where this matter is approached, not from the charitable, but from the patriotic side, there is a tremendous code of legislation for the protection of the men who hold to life by the most uncertain economic tenure. In England there exists an elaborated code of labor laws, protecting the laborer at all times from accidents, in ways unknown in America. Here we have only the beginning of all that legislation, partly because we have not yet broken through the belief that the man who does this casual work is not yet quite one of ourselves. We do not consider him entitled to the protective legislation which is secured for him in other countries where he is quite simply a fellow-citizen, humble it may be, but still bound to the governing class by ties of blood and homogeneity.

Our moral attitude toward one group in the community is a determining factor of our moral attitude toward other groups, and this relation of kindly contempt, of charitable rather than democratic obligation, may lend some explanation to the fact that the United States, as a nation, is sadly in arrears in the legislation designed for the protection of children. In the Southern States, where a contemptuous attitude towards a weaker people has had the most marked effect upon public feeling, we have not only the largest number of unprotected working children, but the largest number of illiterate children as well. There are, in the United States, according to the latest census[1] 580,000 children between the ages of ten and fourteen years, who cannot read nor write. They are not the immigrant children. They are our own native-born children. Of these 570,000 are in the Southern States and ten thousand of them are scattered over the rest of the Republic.

The same thing is true of our children at work. We have two millions of them, according to the census of 1900—children under the age of sixteen years who are earning their own livings.

Legislation of the States south of Maryland for the children is like the legislation of England in 1844. We are sixty-two years behind England in caring for the children of the textile industries.

May we not also trace some of this national indifference to the disposition of the past century to love children without really knowing them? We refuse to recognize them as the great national asset and are content to surround them with a glamour of innocence and charm. We put them prematurely to work, ignorant of the havoc it brings, because no really careful study has been made of their capacities and

---

1. For further analysis of the census figures relating to children, consult "Some Ethical Gains Through Legislation," Mrs. Florence Kelley.

possibilities—that is, no study really fitted to the industrial conditions in which they live.

Each age has, of course, its own temptations and above all its own peculiar industrial temptations and needs to see them not only in the light of the increased sensibility and higher ethical standards of its contemporaries, but also in relation to its peculiar industrial development. When we ask why it is that child-labor has been given to us to discuss and to rectify, rather than to the people who lived before us, we need only to remember that, for the first time in industrial history, the labor of the little child has in many industries become as valuable as that of a man or woman. The old-fashioned weaver was obliged to possess skill and strength to pull his beam back and forth. It is only through the elaborated inventions of our own age that skill as well as strength has been so largely eliminated that, for example, a little child may "tend the thread" in a textile mill almost as well as an adult. This is true of so many industries that the temptation to exploit premature labor has become peculiar to this industrial epoch and we are tempted as never before to use the labor of little children.

What, then, are we going to do about it? How deeply are we concerned that this labor shall not result to the detriment of the child, and what excuses are we making to ourselves for thus prematurely using up the strength which really belongs to the next generation? Of course, it is always difficult to see the wrong in a familiar thing; it is almost a test of moral insight to be able to see that an affair of familiar intercourse and daily living may also be wrong. I have taken a Chicago street-car on a night in December at ten o'clock, when dozens of little girls who had worked in the department stores all day were also boarding the cars. I know, as many others do, that these children will not get into their beds before midnight, and that they will have to be up again early in the morning to go to their daily work. And yet because I have seen it many times I take my car almost placidly—I am happy to say, not quite placidly. Almost every day at six o'clock I see certain factories pouring out a stream of men and women and boys and girls. The boys and girls have a peculiar hue—a color so distinctive that one meeting them on the street, even on Sunday when they are in their best clothes and mingled with other children who go to school and play out of doors, can distinguish them in an instant, and there is on their faces a premature anxiety and sense of responsibility, which we should declare pathetic if we were not used to it.

How far are we responsible when we allow custom to blind our eyes to the things that are wrong? In spite of the enormous growth in charitable and correctional agencies designed for children, are we really so lacking in moral insight and vigor that we fail even to perceive the real temptation of our age and totally fail to grapple with it? An enlightened State which regarded the industrial situation seriously would wish to conserve the ability of its youth, to give them valuable training in relation to industry, quite as the old-fashioned State carefully calculated the years which were the most valuable for military training. The latter, looking only toward the preservation of the State, took infinite pains, while we are careless in regard to the much greater task which has to do with its upbuilding and extension. We conscientiously ignore industry in relation to government and because we assume that its regulation is unnecessary, so we conclude that the protection of the young from premature participation in its mighty operations is not the concern of the Government.

The municipal lodging-house in Chicago in addition to housing vagrants, makes an intelligent effort to put them into regular industry. A physician in attendance makes a careful examination of each man who comes to the lodging-house, and one winter we tried to see what connection could be genuinely established between premature labor and worn-out men. It is surprising to find how many of them are tired to death of monotonous labor, and begin to tramp in order to get away from it—as a business man goes to the woods because he is worn out with the stress of business life. This inordinate desire to get away from work seems to be connected with the fact that the men started to work very early, before they had the physique to stand up to it, or the mental vigor with which to overcome its difficulties, or the moral stamina which makes a man stick to his work whether he likes it or not. But we cannot demand any of these things from the growing boy. They are all traits of the adult. A boy is naturally restless, his determination easily breaks down, and he runs away. At least this seems to be true of many of the men who come to the lodging-house. I recall a man who had begun to work in a textile mill quite below the present legal age in New England, and who had worked hard for sixteen years. He told his tale with all simplicity; and, as he made a motion with his hand, he said, "I done that for sixteen years." I give the words as he gave them. "At last I was sick in bed for two or three weeks with a fever, and when I crawled out, I made up my mind that I would rather go to hell than to go back to that mill." Whether he considered Chicago as equivalent to that, I do not know, but he certainly tramped to Chicago, and has been tramping for four years. He does not steal. He works in a lumber camp occasionally, and wanders about the rest of the time getting odd jobs when he can; but the suggestion of a factory throws him into a panic, and causes him quickly to disappear from the lodging-house. The physician has made a diagnosis of general debility. The man is not fit for steady work. He has been whipped in the battle of life, and is spent prematurely because he began prematurely.

Yet the state makes no careful study as to the effect upon children of the subdivided labor which many of them perform in factories. A child who remains year after year in a spinning room gets no instruction— merely a dull distaste for work. Often he cannot stand up to the grind of factory life, and he breaks down under it.

What does this mean? That we have no right to increase the list of paupers—of those who must be cared for by municipal and State agencies because when they were still immature and undeveloped, they were subjected to a tremendous pressure. I recall one family of five children which, upon the death of the energetic mother who had provided for it by means of a little dress-making establishment, was left to the care of a feeble old grandmother. The father was a drunkard who had never supported his family, and at this time he definitely disappeared. The oldest boy was almost twelve years old—a fine, manly little fellow, who felt keenly his obligation to care for the family.

We found him a place as cash-boy in a department store for two dollars a week. He held it for three years, although his enthusiasm failed somewhat as the months went by, and he gradually discovered how little help his wages were to the family exchequer after his carfare, decent clothes and unending pairs of shoes were paid for. Before the end of the third year he had become listless and indifferent to his work, in spite of the increase of fifty cents a week. In the hope that a change would be good for him, a place as elevator-boy was secured. This he was unable to keep, and then one situation after another slipped through his grasp, until a typhoid fever which he developed at the age of fifteen, seemed to explain his apathy.

After a long illness and a poor recovery, he worked less well. Finally, at the age of sixteen, when he should have been able really to help the little family and perhaps be its main support, he had become a professional tramp, and eventually dropped completely from our knowledge. It was through such bitter lessons as these we learned that good intentions and the charitable impulse do not always work for righteousness; that to force the moral nature of a child and to put tasks upon him beyond his normal growth, is quite as cruel and disastrous as to expect his undeveloped muscle to lift huge weights.

Adolescence is filled with strange pauses of listlessness and dreaminess. At that period the human will is perhaps further away from the desire of definite achievement than it ever is again. To work ten hours a day for six days in a week in order to buy himself a pair of stout boots, that he may be properly shod to go to work some more, is the very last thing which really appeals to a boy of thirteen or fourteen. If he is forced to such a course too often, his cheated nature later reasserts itself in all sorts of decadent and abnormal ways.

An enlightened state would also concern itself with the effect of child labor upon the parents. We have in Chicago a great many European immigrants, people who have come from country life in Bohemia or the south of Italy, hoping that their children will have a better chance here than at home. In the old country these immigrants worked on farms which provided a very normal activity for a young boy or girl. When they come to Chicago, they see no reason why their children should not go to work, because they see no difference between the normal activity of their own youth and the grinding life, to which they subject their children. It is difficult for a man who has grown up in outdoor life to adapt himself to the factory. The same experience is found in the South with the men who come to the textile towns from the little farms. They resent monotonous petty work, and get away from it; they will in preference take more poorly paid work, care of horses or janitor service—work which has some similarity to that to which they have been accustomed. So the parents drop out, and the children, making the adaptation, remain, and the curious result ensues of the head of the household becoming dependent upon the earnings of the child. You will hear a child say, "My mother can't say nothing to me. I pay the rent"; or, "I can do what I please, because I bring home the biggest wages." All this tends to break down the normal relation between parents and children. The Italian men who work on the railroads in the summer find it a great temptation to settle down in the winter upon the wages of their children. A young man from the south of Italy was mourning the death of his little girl of twelve; in his grief he said, quite simply, "She was my oldest kid. In two years she could have supported me, and now I shall have to work five or six years longer until the next one can do it." He expected to retire permanently at thirty-four. That breaking down of the normal relation of parent and child, and the tendency to demoralize the parent, is something we have no right to subject him to. We ought to hold the parent up to the obligation which he would have fulfilled had he remained in his early environment.

A modern state might rightly concern itself with the effect of child labor upon industry itself. There has been for many years an increasing criticism of the modern factory system, not only from the point of view of the worker, but from the point of view of the product itself. It has been said many times that we can not secure good workmanship nor turn out a satisfactory product unless men and women have some sort of interest in their work, and some way of expressing that interest in relation to it. The system which makes no demand upon originality, upon invention, upon self-direction, works automatically, as it were, towards an unintelligent producer and towards an uninteresting product. This was said at first only by such artists and social reformers as Morris and Ruskin; but it is being gradually admitted by men of affairs and may at last incorporate itself into actual factory management, in which case the factory itself will favor child labor legislation or any other measure which increases the free and full development of the individual, because he thereby becomes a more valuable producer. We may gradually discover that in the interests of this industrial society of ours it becomes a distinct loss to put large numbers of producers prematurely at work, not only because the community inevitably loses their mature working power, but also because their "free labor quality," which is so valuable, is permanently destroyed.

Exercise of the instinct of workmanship not only affords great satisfaction to the producer, but also to the consumer, if he be possessed of any critical faculty, or have developed genuine powers of appreciation. Added to the conscience which protests against the social waste of child labor, we have the taste that revolts against a product totally without the charm which pleasure in work creates. We may at last discover that we are imperiling our civilization at the moment of its marked materialism, by wantonly sacrificing to that materialism the eternal spirit of youth, the power of variation, which alone is able to prevent it from degenerating into a mere mechanism.

It would be easy to produce many illustrations to demonstrate that in the leading industrial countries a belief is slowly developing that the workman himself is the chief asset, and that the intelligent interest of skilled men, the power of self-direction and co-operation which is only possible among the free-born and educated, is exactly the only thing which will hold out in the markets of the world. As the foremen of factories testify again and again, factory discipline is valuable only up to a certain point, after which something else must be depended on if the best results are to be achieved.

Monopoly of both the raw material and the newly-opened markets is certainly a valuable factor in a nation's industrial prosperity; but while we spend blood and treasure to protect one and secure the other, we wantonly destroy the most valuable factor of all, intelligent labor. Nothing can help us here save the rising tide of humanitarianism, which is not only emotional enough to regret the pitiless and stupid waste of this power but also intelligent enough to perceive what might be accomplished by its utilization.

We are told that the German products hold a foremost place in the markets of the world because of Germany's fine educational system, which includes training in trade-schools for so many young men. We know, too, that there is at the present moment a strong party in Germany opposing militarism, not from the "peace society" point of view, but because it withdraws all the young men from the industrial life for the best part of three years during which their activity is merely disciplinary, with no relation to the industrial life of the nation. This anti-military party insists that the loss of the three years is a serious matter, and that one nation cannot successfully hold its advance position if it must compete with other nations which are also establishing trade-schools but which do not thus withdraw their youth from continuous training at the period of their greatest docility and aptitude.

England is discovering that the cheap markets afforded by semi-savage peoples, which she has thrown open to her manufacturers, are now reacting in the debasement of her products and her factory workers. The manufacturer produces the cheap and inferior articles which he imagines the new commerce will demand. The result upon the workers in the factories producing these unworthy goods, is that they are robbed of the skill which would be demanded if they were ministering to an increasing demand of taste and if they were supplying the market of a civilized people. It would be a curious result of misapplied energy if those very markets which the Briton has so eagerly sought, would finally so debase the English producers that all the increased wealth the markets have brought to the nation would be consumed in efforts to redeem the debased working population.

We have made public education our great concern in America, and perhaps the public-school system is our most distinctive achievement; but there is a certain lack of consistency in the relation of the State to the child after he leaves the public school. At great expense the State has provided school buildings and equipment, and other buildings in which to prepare professional teachers. It has spared no pains to make the system complete, and yet as rapidly as the children leave the schoolroom, the State seems to lose all interest and responsibility in their welfare and has, until quite recently, turned them over to the employer with no restrictions.

At no point does the community say to the employer, We are allowing you to profit by the labor of these children whom we have educated at great cost, and we demand that they do not work so many hours that they shall be exhausted. Nor shall they be allowed to undertake the sort of labor which is beyond their strength, nor shall they spend their time at work that is absolutely devoid of educational value. The preliminary education which they have received in school is but one step in the process of making them valuable and normal citizens, and we cannot afford to have that intention thwarted, even though the community as well as yourself may profit by the business activity which your factory affords.

Such a position seems perfectly reasonable, yet the same citizens who willingly pay taxes to support an elaborate public-school system, strenuously oppose the most moderate attempts to guard the children from needless and useless exploitation after they have left school and have entered industry.

We are forced to believe that child labor is a national problem, even as public education is a national duty. The children of Alabama, Rhode Island, and Pennsylvania belong to the nation quite as much as they belong to each State, and the nation has an interest in the children at least in relation to their industrial efficiency, quite as it has an interest in enacting protective tariffs for the preservation of American industries.

Uniform compulsory education laws in connection with uniform child labor legislation are the important factors in securing educated producers for the nation. Fortunately, a new education is arising which endeavors to widen and organize the child's experience with reference to the world in which he lives.[2] The new pedagogy holds that it is a child's instinct and pleasure to exercise all his faculties and to make discoveries in the world around him. It is the chief business of the teacher merely to direct his activity and to feed his insatiable curiosity. In order to accomplish this, he is forced to relate the child to the surroundings in which he lives; and the most advanced schools are, perforce, using modern industry for this purpose. The educators have ceased to mourn industrial conditions of the past generation, when children were taught agricultural and industrial arts by the natural cooperation with their parents, and they are endeavoring to supply this inadequacy by manual arts in the school, by courses in industrial history and by miniature reproductions of industrial processes, thus constantly coming into better relations with the present factory system. These educators recognize the significance and power of contemporary industrialism, and hold it an obligation to protect children from premature participation in our industrial life, only that the children may secure the training and fibre which will later make this participation effective, and that their minds may finally take possession of the machines which they will guide and feed.

But there is another side to the benefits of child-labor legislation rep-

2. *School and Society,* by John Dewey.

resented by the time element, the leisure which is secured to the child for the pursuit of his own affairs, quite aside from the opportunity afforded him to attend school. Helplessness in childhood, the scientists tell us, is the guarantee of adult intellect, but they also assert that play in youth is the guarantee of adult culture. It is the most valuable instrument the race possesses to keep life from becoming mechanical.

The child who cannot live life is prone to dramatize it, and the very process is a constant compromise between imitation and imagination, as the over-mastering impulse itself which drives him to incessant play is both reminiscent and anticipatory. In proportion as the child in later life is to be subjected to a mechanical and one-sided activity, and as a highly subdivided labor is to be demanded from him, it is therefore most important that he should have his full period of childhood and youth for this play expression in order that he may cultivate within himself the root of a culture which alone can give his later activity a meaning.[3] This is true whether or not we accept the theory that the aesthetic feelings originate in the play impulse, with its corollary that the constant experimentation found in the commonest forms of play are to be looked upon as "the principal source of all kinds of art." At this moment, when industrial forces are concentrated and unified as never before, unusual care must be taken to secure to the children their normal play period, that the art instinct may have some chance, and that the producer himself may have enough individuality of character to avoid becoming a mere cog in the vast industrial machine.

Quite aside also from the problem of individual development and from the fact that play, in which the power of choice is constantly presented and constructive imagination required, is the best corrective of the future disciplinary life of the factory, there is another reason why the children who are to become producers under the present system should be given their full child-life period.

The entire population of the factory town and of those enormous districts in every large city in which the children live who most need the protection of child-labor legislation, consists of people who have come together in response to the demands of modern industry. They are held together by the purely impersonal tie of working in one large

3. *The Play of Man,* Groos, page 394.

factory, in which they not only do not know each other, but in which no one person nor even group of persons knows everybody. They are utterly without the natural and minute acquaintance and inter-family relationships that rural and village life afford, and are therefore much more dependent upon the social sympathy and power of effective association which is becoming its urban substitute.

This substitute can be most easily elaborated among groups of children. Somewhere they must learn to carry on an orderly daily life—that life of mutual trust, forbearance, and help which is the only real life of civilized man. Play is the great social stimulus, and it is the prime motive which unites children and draws them into comradeship. A true democratic relation and ease of acquaintance is found among the children in a typical factory community because they more readily overcome differences of language, tradition, and religion than do the adults. "It is in play that nature reveals her anxious care to discover men to each other," and this happy and important task, children unconsciously carry forward day by day with all the excitement and joy of co-ordinate activity. They accomplish that which their elders could not possibly do, and they render a most important service to the community. We have not as yet utilized this joy of association in relation to the system of factory production which is so preeminently one of large bodies of men working together for hours at a time. But there is no doubt that it would bring a new power into modern industry if the factory could avail itself of that *esprit de corps,* that triumphant buoyancy which the child experiences when he feels his complete identification with a social group; that sense of security which comes upon him sitting in a theatre or "at a party," when he issues forth from himself and is lost in a fairyland which has been evoked not only by his own imagination, but by that of his companions as well. This power of association, of assimilation, which children possess in such a high degree, is easily carried over into the affairs of youth if it but be given opportunity and freedom for action, as it is in the college life of more favored young people. The *esprit de corps* of an athletic team, that astonishing force of co-operation, is, however, never consciously carried over into industry, but is persistently disregarded. It is, indeed, lost before it is discovered—if I may be permitted an Irish bull—in the case of children who are put to work before they have had time to develop the power beyond its most childish and haphazard manifestations.

Factory life depends upon groups of people working together, and yet it is content with the morphology of the group, as it were, paying no attention to its psychology, to the interaction of its members. By regarding each producer as a solitary unit, a tremendous power is totally unutilized. In the case of children who are prematurely put to work under such conditions, an unwarranted nervous strain is added as they make their effort to stand up to the individual duties of life while still in the stage of group and family dependence.

We naturally associate a factory with orderly productive action; but similarity of action, without identical thought and co-operative intelligence, is coercion, and not order. The present factory discipline needs to be redeemed as the old school discipline has been redeemed. In the latter the system of prizes and punishments has been largely given up, not only because they were difficult to administer, but because they utterly failed to free the powers of the child.

"The fear of starvation," of which the old economists made so much, is, after all, but a poor incentive to work; and the appeal to cupidity by which a man is induced to "speed up" in all the various devices of piece-work is very little better. Yet the factory still depends upon these as incentives to the ordinary workers. Certainly one would wish to protect children from them as long as possible. In a soap factory in Chicago little girls wrap bars of soap in two covers at the minimum rate of 3,000 bars a week; their only ambition is to wrap as fast as possible and well enough to pass the foreman's inspection. The girl whose earnings are the largest at the end of the week is filled with pride—praiseworthy certainly, but totally without educational value.

Let us realize before it is too late that in this age of iron, of machine-tending, and of subdivided labor, we need as never before the untrammeled and inspired activity of youth. To cut it off from thousands of working children is a most perilous undertaking, and endangers the very industry to which they have been sacrificed.

Only of late years has an effort been made by the city authorities, by the municipality itself, to conserve the play instinct and to utilize it, if not for the correction of industry, at least for the nurture of citizenship. It has been discovered that the city which is too careless to provide playgrounds, gymnasiums, and athletic fields where the boys legitimately belong and which the policeman is bound to respect, simply puts a premium on lawlessness. Without these places of their own, groups of boys come to look upon the policeman as an enemy, and he regards them as the most lawless of all the citizens. This is partly due to the fact that because of our military survivals the officer is not brought in contact with the educational forces of the city, but only with its vices and crime. He might have quite as great an opportunity for influencing the morals of youth as the school teacher has. At least one American city spends twenty per cent more in provision for the conviction of youths than for their education, for the city which fails to utilize this promising material of youthful adventure does not truly get rid of it, and finds it more expensive to care for as waste material than as educative material. At a certain age a boy is possessed by a restless determination to do something dangerous and exciting—a "difficult stunt," as it were—by which he may prove that he is master of his fate and thus express his growing self-assertion. He prefers to demonstrate in feats requiring both courage and adroitness, and it may be said that tradition is with him in his choice. That this impulse is mixed with an absurd desire on the part of the boy to "show off," to impress his companions with the fact that he is great and brave and generally to be admired, does not in the least affect its genuineness. The city which fails to provide an opportunity for this inevitable and normal desire on the part of the young citizens makes a grave mistake and invites irregular expression of it. The thwarted spirit of adventure finds an outlet in infinite varieties of gambling; craps, cards, the tossing of discarded union buttons, the betting on odd or even automobile numbers, on the number of newspapers under a boy's arm. Another end which can be accomplished, if the city recognizes play as legitimate and provides playgrounds and athletic fields, is the development of that self-government and self-discipline among groups of boys, which forms the most natural basis for democratic political life later.

The boy in a tenement-house region who does not belong to the gang is not only an exception, but a very rare exception. This earliest form of social life is almost tribal in its organization, and the leader too often holds his place because he is a successful bully. The gang meets first upon the street, but later it may possess a club room in a stable, in a billiard room, in an empty house, under the viaduct, in a candy store, in a saloon or even in an empty lot. The spirit of association, the fellowship and loyalty which the group inspires, carry them into many dangers; but there is no doubt that it is through these experiences that the city boy learns his political lessons. The training for political life is given in these gangs, and also an opportunity to develop that wonderful power of adaptation which is the city's contribution, even to the poorest of her children. A clever man once told me that he doubted whether an alderman could be elected in a tenement-house district unless he had had gang experience, and had become an adept in the interminable discussion which every detail of the gang's activity receives. This alone affords a training in democratic government, for it is the prerogative of democracy to invest political discussion with the dignity of deeds, and to provide adequate motives for discussion. In these social folk-motes, so to speak, the young citizen learns to act upon his own determination. The great pity is that it so often results in a group morality untouched by a concern for the larger morality of the community. Normal groups reacting upon each other would tend to an equilibrium of a certain liberty to all, but this cannot be accomplished in the life of the street where the weaker boy or the weaker gang is continually getting the worst of it. And it is only on the protected playground that the gangs can be merged into baseball nines and similar organizations, governed by well-recognized rules.

We have already democratized education in the interests of the entire community; but recreation and constructive play, which afford the best soil for establishing genuine and democratic social relations, we have left untouched, although they are so valuable in emotional and dynamic power. Further than that, the city that refrains from educating the play motive is obliged to suppress it. In Chicago gangs of boys between fourteen and sixteen years of age, who, possessing work-certificates are outside of the jurisdiction of the truant officer, are continually being arrested by the police, since they have no orderly opportunity for recreation. An enlightened city government would regard these groups of boys as the natural soil in which to sow the seeds of self-government. As every European city has its parade-ground, where the mimics of war are faithfully rehearsed, in order that the country may be saved in times of danger, so, if modern government were as really concerned in developing its citizens as it is in defending them, we would look upon every playing-field as the training-place and parade-ground of mature citizenship.

Frederick the Great discovered and applied the use of the rhythmic step for the marching of soldiers. For generations men had gone forth to war, using martial music as they had used the battle-cry, merely to incite their courage and war spirit; but the music had had nothing to do with their actual marching. The use of it as a practical measure enormously increased the endurance of the soldiers and raised the records of forced marches. Industry at the present moment, as represented by masses of men in the large factories, is quite as chaotic as the early armies were. We have failed to apply our education to the real life of the average factory producer. He works without any inner coherence or sense of comradeship. Our public education has done little as yet to release his powers or to cheer him with the knowledge of his significance to the State.

VII

Utilization of Women in City Government

We are told many times that the industrial city is a new thing upon the face of the earth, and that everywhere its growth has been phenomenal, whether we look at Moscow, Berlin, Paris, New York, or Chicago. With or without the mediaeval foundation, modern cities are merely resultants of the vast crowds of people who have collected at certain points which have become manufacturing and distributing centres.

For all political purposes, however, the industrial origin of the city is entirely ignored, and political life is organized exclusively in relation to its earlier foundations.

As the city itself originated for the common protection of the people and was built about a suitable centre of defense which formed a citadel, such as the Acropolis at Athens or the Kremlin at Moscow, so we can trace the beginning of the municipal franchise to the time when the problems of municipal government were still largely those of protecting the city against rebellion from within and against invasion from without. A voice in city government, as it was extended from the nobles, who alone bore arms, was naturally given solely to those who were valuable to the military system. There was a certain logic in giving the franchise only to grown men when the existence and stability of the city depended upon their defence, and when the ultimate value of the elector could be reduced to his ability to perform military duty. It was fair that only those who were liable to a sudden call to arms should be selected to decide as to the relations which the city should bear to rival cities, and that the vote for war should be cast by the same men who would bear the brunt of battle and the burden of protection. We are told by historians that the citizens were first called together in those assemblages which were the beginning of popular government, only if a war was to be declared or an expedition to be undertaken.

But rival cities have long since ceased to settle their claims by force of arms, and we shall have to admit, I think, that this early test of the elector is no longer fitted to the modern city, whatever may be true, in the last analysis, of the basis for the Federal Government.

It has been well said that the modern city is a stronghold of industrialism, quite as the feudal city was a stronghold of militarism, but the modern city fears no enemies, and rivals from without and its problems of government are solely internal. Affairs for the most part are going badly in these great new centres in which the quickly congregated population has not yet learned to arrange its affairs satisfactorily. Insanitary housing, poisonous sewage, contaminated water, infant mortality, the spread of contagion, adulterated food, impure milk, smoke-laden air, ill-ventilated factories, dangerous occupations, juvenile crime, unwholesome crowding, prostitution, and drunkenness are the enemies which the modern city must face and overcome would it survive. Logically, its electorate should be made up of those who can bear a valiant part in this arduous contest, of those who in the past have at least attempted to care for children, to clean houses, to prepare foods, to isolate the family from moral dangers, of those who have traditionally taken care of that side of life which, as soon as the population is congested, inevitably becomes the subject of municipal consideration and control.

To test the elector's fitness to deal with this situation by his ability to bear arms, is absurd. A city is in many respects a great business corporation, but in other respects it is enlarged housekeeping. If American cities have failed in the first, partly because office holders have carried with them the predatory instinct learned in competitive business, and cannot help "working a good thing" when they have an opportunity, may we not say that city housekeeping has failed partly because women, the traditional housekeepers, have not been consulted as to its multiform activities? The men of the city have been carelessly indifferent to much of this civic housekeeping, as they have always been indifferent to the details of the household. They have totally disregarded a candidate's capacity to keep the streets clean, preferring to consider him in relation to the national tariff or to the necessity for increasing the national navy, in a pure spirit of reversion to the traditional type of government which had to do only with enemies and outsiders.

It is difficult to see what military prowess has to do with the multiform duties, which, in a modern city, include the care of parks and libraries, superintendence of markets, sewers, and bridges, the inspection of provisions and boilers, and the proper disposal of garbage. Military prowess has nothing to do with the building department which the city maintains to see to it that the basements be dry, that the bedrooms be large enough to afford the required cubic feet of air, that the plumbing be sanitary, that the gas-pipes do not leak, that the tenement-house court be large enough to afford light and ventilation, and that the stairways be fireproof. The ability to carry arms has nothing to do with the health department maintained by the city, which provides that children be vaccinated, that contagious diseases be isolated and placarded, that the spread of tuberculosis be curbed, and that the water be free from typhoid infection. Certainly the military conception of society is remote from the functions of the school boards, whose concern it is that children be educated, that they be supplied with kindergartens and be given a decent place in which to play. The very multifariousness and complexity of a city government demands the help of minds accustomed to detail and variety of work, to a sense of obligation for the health and welfare of young children, and to a responsibility for the cleanliness and comfort of others.

Because all these things have traditionally been in the hands of women, if they take no part in them now, they are not only missing the education which the natural participation in civic life would bring to them, but they are losing what they have always had. From the beginning of tribal life women have been held responsible for the health of the community, a function which is now represented by the health department; from the days of the cave dwellers, so far as the home was clean and wholesome, it was due to their efforts, which are now represented by the bureau of tenement-house inspection; from the period of the primitive village, the only public sweeping performed was what they undertook in their own dooryards, that which is now represented by the bureau of street cleaning. Most of the departments in a modern city can be traced to woman's traditional activity, but in spite of this, so soon as these old affairs were turned over to the care of the city, they slipped from woman's hands, apparently because they then became matters for collective action and implied the use of the franchise. Because the franchise had in the first instance been given to the man who could fight, because in the beginning he alone could vote who could carry a weapon, the franchise was considered an improper thing for a woman to possess.

Is it quite public spirited for women to say, "We will take care of these affairs so long as they stay in our own houses, but if they go outside and concern so many people that they cannot be carried on without the mechanism of the vote, we will drop them. It is true that these activities which women have always had, are not at present being carried on very well by the men in most of the great American cities, but because we do not consider it 'ladylike' to vote shall we ignore their failure"?

Because women consider the government men's affair and something which concerns itself with elections and alarms, they have become so confused in regard to their traditional business in life, the rearing of children, that they hear with complacency a statement made by the Nestor of sanitary reformers, that one-half of the tiny lives which make up the city's death rate each year might be saved by a more thorough application of sanitary science. Because it implies the use of the suffrage, they do not consider it women's business to save these lives. Are we going to lose ourselves in the old circle of convention and add to that sum of wrong-doing which is continually committed in the world because we do not look at things as they really are? Old-fashioned ways which no longer apply to changed conditions are a snare in which the feet of women have always become readily entangled. It is so easy to believe that things that used to exist still go on long after they are passed; it is so easy to commit irreparable blunders because we fail to correct our theories by our changing experience. So many of the stumbling-blocks against which we fall are the opportunities to which we have not adjusted ourselves. Because it shocks an obsolete ideal, we keep hold of a convention which no longer squares with our genuine insight, and we are slow to follow a clue which might enable us to solace and improve the life about us.

Why is it that women do not vote upon the matters which concern them so intimately? Why do they not follow these vital affairs and feel responsible for their proper administration, even though they have become municipalized? What would the result have been could women have regarded the suffrage, not as a right or a privilege, but as a mere piece of governmental machinery without which they could not perform their traditional functions under the changed conditions of city life? Could we view the whole situation as a matter of obligation and of normal development, it would be much simplified. We are at the beginning of a prolonged effort to incorporate a progressive developing life founded upon a response to the needs of all the people, into the requisite legal enactments and civic institutions. To be in any measure successful, this effort will require all the intelligent powers of observation, all the sympathy, all the common sense which may be gained from the whole adult population.

The statement is sometimes made that the franchise for women would be valuable only so far as the educated women exercised it. This statement totally disregards the fact that those matters in which woman's judgment is most needed are far too primitive and basic to be largely influenced by what we call education. The sanitary condition of all the factories and workshops, for instance, in which the industrial processes are at present carried on in great cities, intimately affect the health and lives of thousands of workingwomen.

It is questionable whether women to-day, in spite of the fact that there are myriads of them in factories and shops, are doing their full share of the world's work in the lines of production which have always been theirs. Even two centuries ago they did practically all the spinning, dyeing, weaving, and sewing. They carried on much of the brewing and baking and thousands of operations which have been pushed out of the domestic system into the factory system. But simply to keep on doing the work which their grandmothers did, was to find themselves surrounded by conditions over which they have no control.

Sometimes when I see dozens of young girls going into the factories of a certain biscuit company on the West Side of Chicago, they appear for the moment as a mere cross-section in the long procession of women who have furnished the breadstuffs from time immemorial, from the savage woman who ground the meal and baked a flat cake, through innumerable cottage hearths, kitchens, and bake ovens, to this huge concern in which they are still carrying on their traditional business. But always before, during the ages of this unending procession, women themselves were able to dictate concerning the hours and the immediate conditions of their work; even grinding the meal and baking the cake in the ashes was diversified by many other activities. But suddenly, since the application of steam to the processes of kneading bread and of turning the spindle, which really means only a different motor power and not in the least an essential change in her work, she has been denied the privilege of regulating the conditions which immediately surround her.

In the census of 1900, the section on "Occupations" shows very clearly in what direction the employment of women has been tending during the last twenty years. Two striking facts stand out vividly: first, the increase in the percentage of workingwomen over the percentage of men, and second, the large percentage of young women between sixteen and twenty years old in the total number of workingwomen as compared with the small percentage of young men of the same ages in the total number of workingmen. Practically one-half of the workingwomen in the United States are girls—young women under the age of twenty-five years. This increase in the number of young girls in industry is the more striking when taken in connection with the fact that industries of to-day differ most markedly from those of the past in the relentless speed which they require. This increase in speed is as marked in the depths of sweat-shop labor as in the most advanced New England mills, where the eight looms operated by each worker have increased to twelve, fourteen, and even sixteen looms. This speed, of course, brings a new strain into industry and tends inevitably to nervous exhaustion. Machines may be revolved more and more swiftly, but the girl workers have no increase in vitality responding to the heightened pressure. An ampler and more far-reaching protection than now exists, is needed in order to care for the health and safety of women in industry. Their youth, their helplessness, their increasing numbers, the conditions under which they are employed, all call for uniform and enforceable statutes. The elaborate regulations of dangerous trades, enacted in England and on the Continent for both adults and children, find no parallel in the United States. The injurious effects of employments involving the use of poisons, acids, gases, atmospheric extremes, or other dangerous processes, still await adequate investigation and legislation in this country. How shall this take place, save by the concerted efforts of the women themselves, those who are employed, and those other women who are intelligent as to the worker's needs and who possess a conscience in regard to industrial affairs?

It is legitimate and necessary that women should make a study of certain trades and occupations. The production of sweated goods, from the human point of view, is not production at all, but waste. If the employer takes from the workers week by week more than his wages restore to them, he gradually reduces them to the state of industrial parasites. The wages of the sweated worker are either being supplemented by the wages of relatives and the gifts of charitable associations, or else her standard of living is so low that she is continually losing her vitality and tending to become a charge upon the community in a hospital or a poorhouse.[1]

Yet even the sweat-shops, in which woman carries on her old business of making clothing, had to be redeemed, so far as they have been redeemed, by the votes of men who passed an anti-sweat-shop law; by the city fathers, who, after much pleading, were induced to order an inspection of sweat-shops that they might be made to comply with sanitary regulations. Women directly controlled the surroundings of their work as long as their arrangements were domestic, but they cannot do this now unless they have the franchise, as yet the only mechanism devised by which a city selects its representative and by which a number of persons are able to embody their collective will in legislation. For a hundred years England has been legislating upon the subject of insanit[ar]y workshops, long and exhausting hours of work, night work for women, occupations in which pregnant women may be employed, and hundreds of other restrictions which we are only beginning to consider objects of legislation here.

So far as women have been able, in Chicago at least, to help the poorest workers in the sweat-shops, it has been accomplished by women organized into trades unions. The organization of Special Order Tailors found that it was comparatively simple for an employer to give the skilled operatives in a clothing factory more money by taking it away from the wages of the seam-sewer and button-holer. The fact that it

1. *A Case for the Factory Acts,* Mrs. Sidney Webb.

resulted in one set of workers being helped at the expense of another set did not appeal to him, so long as he was satisfying the demand of the union without increasing the total cost of production. But the Special Order Tailors, at the sacrifice of their own wages and growth, made a determined effort to include even the sweat-shop workers in the benefits they had slowly secured for themselves. By means of the use of the label they were finally able to insist that no goods should be given out for home-finishing save to women presenting union cards, and they raised the wages from nine and eleven cents a dozen for finishing garments, to the minimum wage of fifteen cents. They also made a protest against the excessive subdivision of the labor upon garments, a practice which enables the manufacturer to use children and the least skilled adults. Thirty-two persons are commonly employed upon a single coat, and it is the purpose of the Special Order Tailors to have all the machine work performed by one worker, thus reducing the number working on one coat to twelve or fourteen. As this change will at the same time demand more skill on the part of the operator, and will increase the variety and interest in his work, these garment-makers are sacrificing both time and money for the defence of Ruskinian principles—one of the few actual attempts to recover the "joy of work." Although the attempt was, of course, mixed with a desire to preserve a trade from the invasion of the unskilled, and a consequent lowering of wages, it also represented a genuine effort to preserve to the poorest worker some interest and value in the work itself. It is most unfair, however, to put this task upon the trades unionists and to so confuse it with their other efforts that it, too, becomes a cause of warfare. The poorest women are often but uncomprehending victims of this labor movement of which they understand so little, and which has become so much a matter of battle that helpless individuals are lost in the conflict.

A complicated situation occurs to me in illustration. A woman from the Hull-House Day Nursery came to me two years ago asking to borrow twenty-five dollars, a sum her union had imposed as a fine. She gave such an incoherent account of her plight that it was evident that she did not in the least understand what it was all about. A little investigation disclosed the following facts: The "Nursery Mother," as I here call her for purposes of identification, had worked for a long time in an unorganized overall factory, where the proprietor, dealing as he did in goods purchased exclusively by workingmen, found it increasingly difficult to sell his overalls because they did not bear the union label. He finally made a request to the union that the employees in his factory be organized. This was done, he was given the use of the label, and upon this basis he prospered for several months.

Whether the organizer was "fixed" or not, the investigation did not make clear; for, although the "Nursery Mother," with her fellow-workers, had paid their union dues regularly, the employer was not compelled to pay the union scale of wages, but continued to pay the same wages as before. At the end of three months his employees discovered that they were not being paid the union scale, and demanded that their wages be raised to that amount. The employer, in the meantime having extensively advertised his use of the label, concluded that his purpose had been served, and that he no longer needed the union. He refused, therefore, to pay the union scale, and a strike ensued. The "Nursery Mother" went out with the rest, and within a few days found work in another shop, a union shop doing a lower grade of manufacturing. At that time there was no uniform scale in the garment trades, and although a trade unionist working for union wages, she received lower wages than she had under the non-union conditions in the overall factory. She was naturally much confused and, following her instinct to get the best wages possible, she went back to her old place. Affairs ran smoothly for a few weeks, until the employer discovered that he was again losing trade because his goods lacked the label, whereupon he once more applied to have his shop unionized. The organizer, coming back, promptly discovered the recreant "Nursery Mother," and, much to her bewilderment, she was fined twenty-five dollars. She understood nothing clearly; nor could she, indeed, be made to understand so long as she was in the midst of this petty warfare. Her labor was a mere method of earning money quite detached from her European experience, and failed to make for her the remotest connection with the community whose genuine needs she was supplying. No effort had been made to show her the cultural aspect of her work, to give her even the feeblest understanding of the fact that she was supplying a genuine need of the community, and that she was entitled to respect and a legitimate industrial position. It would have been necessary to make such an effort from the historic standpoint, and this could be undertaken only by the community as a whole and not by any one class in it. Protective legislation would be but the first step toward making her a more valuable producer and a more intelligent citizen. The whole effort would imply a closer connection between industry and government, and could be accomplished intelligently only if women were permitted to exercise the franchise.

A certain healing and correction would doubtless ensue could we but secure for the protection and education of industrial workers that nurture of health and morals which women have so long reserved for their own families and which has never been utilized as a directing force in industrial affairs.

When the family constituted the industrial organism of the day, the daughters of the household were carefully taught in reference to the place they would take in that organism, but as the household arts have gone outside the home, almost nothing has been done to connect the young women with the present great industrial system. This neglect has been equally true in regard to the technical and cultural sides of that system.

The failure to fit the education of women to the actual industrial life which is carried on about them has had disastrous results in two directions. First, industry itself has lacked the modification which women might have brought to it had they committed the entire movement to that growing concern for a larger and more satisfying life for each member of the community, a concern which we have come to regard as legitimate. Second, the more prosperous women would have been able to understand and adjust their own difficulties of household management in relation to the producer of factory products, as they are now utterly unable to do.

As the census of 1900 showed that more than half of the women employed in "gainful occupations" in the United States are engaged in households, certainly their conditions of labor lie largely in the hands of women employers. At a conference held at Lake Placid by employers of household labor, it was contended that future historical review may show that the girls who are to-day in domestic service are the really progressive women of the age; that they are those who are fighting conditions which limit their freedom, and although they are doing it blindly, at least they are demanding avenues of self-expression outside their work; and that this struggle from conditions detrimental to their highest life is the ever-recurring story of the emancipation of first one class and then another. It was further contended that in this effort to become sufficiently educated to be able to understand the needs of an educated employer from an independent standpoint, they are really doing the community a great service, and did they but receive co-operation instead of opposition, domestic service would lose its social ostracism and attract a more intelligent class of women. And yet this effort, perfectly reasonable from the standpoint of historic development and democratic tradition, receives little help from the employing housekeepers, because they know nothing of industrial development.

The situation could be understood only by viewing it, first, in the relation to recent immigration and, second, in connection with the factory system at the present stage of development in America. A review of the history of domestic service in a fairly prosperous American family begins with the colonial period, when the daughters of the neighboring farmers came in to "help" during the busy season. This was followed by the Irish immigrant, when almost every kitchen had its Nora or Bridget, while the mistress of the household retained the sweeping and dusting and the Saturday baking. Then came the halcyon days of German "second girls" and cooks, followed by the Swedes. The successive waves of immigration supply the demand for domestic service, gradually obliterating the fact that as the women became more familiar with American customs, they as well as their men folk, entered into more skilled and lucrative positions.

In these last years immigration consists in ever-increasing numbers of South Italians and of Russian, Polish, and Rumanian Jews, none of whom have to any appreciable extent entered into domestic service. The Italian girls are married between the ages of fifteen and eighteen, and to live in any house in town other than that of her father seems to an Italian girl quite incomprehensible. The strength of the family tie, the need for "kosher" foods, the celebration of religious festivities, the readiness with which she takes up the sewing trades in which her father and brother are already largely engaged, makes domestic service a rare occupation for the daughters of the recent Jewish immigrants. Moreover, these two classes of immigrants have been quickly absorbed, as, indeed, all working people are, by the increasing demand for the labor of young girls and children in factory and workshops. The paucity of the material for domestic service is therefore revealed at last, and we are obliged to consider the material for domestic service which a democracy supplies, and also to realize that the administration of the household has suffered because it has become unnaturally isolated from the rest of the community.

The problems of food and shelter for the family, at any given moment, must be considered in relation to all the other mechanical and industrial life of that moment, quite as the intellectual life of the family finally depends for its vitality upon its relation to the intellectual resources of the rest of the community. When the administrator of the household deliberately refuses to avail herself of the wonderful inventions going on all about her, she soon comes to the point of priding herself upon the fact that her household is administered according to traditional lines and of believing that the moral life of the family is so enwrapped in these old customs as to be endangered by any radical change. Because of this attitude on the part of contemporary housekeepers, the household has firmly withstood the beneficent changes and healing innovations which applied science and economics would long ago have brought about could they have worked naturally and unimpeded.

These moral and economic difficulties, whether connected with the isolation of the home or with the partial and unsatisfactory efforts of trades unions, could be avoided only if society would frankly recognize the industrial situation as that which concerns us all, and would seriously prepare all classes of the community for their relation to the situation. A technical preparation would, of course, not be feasible, but a cultural one would be possible, so that all parts of the community might be intelligent in regard to the industrial developments and transitions going about them. If American women could but obtain a liberating knowledge of that history of industry and commerce which is so similar in every country of the globe, the fact that so much factory labor is performed by immigrants would help to bring them nearer to the immigrant woman. Equipped with "the informing mind" on the one hand and with experience on the other, we could then walk together through the marvelous streets of the human city, no longer conscious whether we are natives or aliens, because we have become absorbed in a fraternal relation arising from a common experience.

And this attitude of understanding and respect for the worker is necessary, not only to appreciate what he produces, but to preserve his power of production, again showing the necessity for making that substitute for war—human labor—more aggressive and democratic. We are told that the conquered races everywhere, in their helplessness, are giving up the genuine practise of their own arts. In India, for instance, where their arts have been the blossom of many years of labor, the conquered races are casting them aside as of no value in order that they may conform to the inferior art, or rather, lack of art, of their conquerors. Morris constantly lamented that in some parts of India the native arts were quite destroyed, and in many others nearly so; that in all parts they had more or less begun to sicken. This lack of respect and understanding of the primitive arts found among colonies of immigrants in a modern cosmopolitan city, produces a like result in that the arts languish and disappear. We have made an effort at Hull-House to recover something of the early industries from an immigrant neighborhood, and in a little exhibit called a labor museum, we have placed in historic sequence and order methods of spinning and weaving from a dozen nationalities in Asia Minor and Europe. The result has been a striking exhibition of the unity and similarity of the earlier industrial processes. Within the narrow confines of one room, the Syrian, the Greek, the Italian, the Russian, the Norwegian, the Dutch, and the Irish find that the differences in their spinning have been merely putting the distaff upon a frame or placing the old hand-spindle in a horizontal position. A group of women representing vast differences in religion, in language, in tradition, and in nationality, exhibit practically no difference in the daily arts by which, for a thousand generations, they have clothed their families. When American women come to visit them, the quickest method, in fact almost the only one of establishing a genuine companionship with them, is through this same industry, unless we except that still older occupation, the care of little children. Perhaps this experiment may claim to have made a genuine effort to find the basic experiences upon which a cosmopolitan community may unite at least on the industrial side. The recent date of the industrial revolution and our nearness to a primitive industry are shown by the fact that Italian mothers are more willing to have their daughters work in factories producing textile and food stuffs than in those which produce wood and metal. They interpret the entire situation so simply that it appears to them just what it is—a mere continuation of woman's traditional work under changed conditions. Another example of our nearness to early methods is shown by the fact that many women from South Italy and from the remoter parts of Russia have never seen a spinning-wheel, and look upon it as a new and marvelous invention. But these very people, who are habitually at such a disadvantage because they lack certain superficial qualities which are too highly prized, have an opportunity in the labor museum, at least for the moment, to assert a position in the community to which their previous life and training entitles them, and they are judged with something of a historic background. Their very apparent remoteness gives industrial processes a picturesque content and charm.

Can we learn our first lesson in modern industry from these humble peasant women who have never shirked the primitive labors upon which all civilized life is founded, even as we must obtain our first lessons in social morality from those who are bearing the brunt of the overcrowded and cosmopolitan city which is the direct result of modern industrial conditions? If we contend that the franchise should be extended to women on the ground that less emphasis is continually placed upon the military order and more upon the industrial order of society, we should have to insist that, if she would secure her old place in industry, the modern woman must needs fit her labors to the present industrial organization as the simpler woman fitted hers to the more simple industrial order. It has been pointed out that woman lost her earlier place when man usurped the industrial pursuits and created wealth on a scale unknown before. Since that time women have been reduced more and more to a state of dependency, until we see only among the European peasant women as they work in the fields, "the heavy, strong, enduring, patient, economically functional representative of what the women of our day used to be."

Cultural education as it is at present carried on in the most advanced schools, is to some extent correcting the present detached relation of women to industry but a sense of responsibility in relation to the development of industry would accomplish much more. As men earned their citizenship through their readiness and ability to defend their city, so perhaps woman, if she takes a citizen's place in the modern industrial city, will have to earn it by devotion and self-abnegation in the service of its complex needs.

The old social problems were too often made a cause of war in the belief that all difficulties could be settled by an appeal to arms. But certainly these subtler problems which confront the modern cosmopolitan city, the problems of race antagonisms and economic adjustments, must be settled by a more searching and genuine method than mere prowess can possibly afford. The first step toward their real solution must be made upon a past experience common to the citizens as a whole and connected with their daily living. As moral problems become more and more associated with our civic and industrial organizations, the demand for enlarged activity is more exigent. If one could connect the old maternal anxieties, which are really the basis of family and tribal life, with the candidates who are seeking offices, it would never be necessary to look about for other motive powers, and if to this we could add maternal concern for the safety and defence of the industrial worker, we should have an increasing code of protective legislation.

We certainly may hope for two results if women enter formally into municipal life. First, the opportunity to fulfill their old duties and obligations with the safeguard and the consideration which the ballot alone can secure for them under the changed conditions, and, second, the education which participation in actual affairs always brings. As we believe that woman has no right to allow what really belongs to her to drop away from her, so we contend that ability to perform an obligation comes very largely in proportion as that obligation is conscientiously assumed.

Out of the mediaeval city founded upon militarism there arose in the thirteenth century a new order, the middle class, whose importance rested, not upon birth or arms, but upon wealth, intelligence, and organization. This middle class achieved a sterling success in the succeeding six centuries of industrialism because it was essential to the existence and development of the industrial era. Perhaps we can forecast the career of woman, the citizen, if she is permitted to bear an elector's part in the coming period of humanitarianism in which government must concern itself with human welfare. She will bear her share of civic responsibility because she is essential to the normal development of the city of the future, and because the definition of the loyal citizen as one who is ready to shed his blood for his country, has become inadequate and obsolete.

VIII

Passing of the War Virtues

 Of all the winged words which Tolstoy wrote during the war between Russia and Japan, perhaps none are more significant than these: "The great strife of our time is not that now taking place between the Japanese and the Russians, nor that which may blaze up between the white and the yellow races, nor that strife which is carried on by mines, bombs, and bullets, but that spiritual strife which, without ceasing, has gone on and is going on between the enlightened consciousness of mankind now awaiting for manifestation and that darkness and that burden which surrounds and oppresses mankind." In the curious period of accommodation in which we live, it is possible for old habits and new compunctions to be equally powerful, and it is almost a matter of pride with us that we neither break with the old nor yield to the new. We call this attitude tolerance, whereas it is often mere confusion of mind. Such mental confusion is strikingly illustrated by our tendency to substitute a statement of the historic evolution of an ideal of conduct in place of the ideal itself. This almost always occurs when the ideal no longer accords with our faithful experience of life and when its implications are not justified by our latest information. In this way we spare ourselves the necessity of pressing forward to newer ideals of conduct.

We quote the convictions and achievements of the past as an excuse for ourselves when we lack the energy either to throw off old moral codes which have become burdens or to attain a morality proportionate to our present sphere of activity.

At the present moment the war spirit attempts to justify its noisy demonstrations by quoting its great achievements in the past and by drawing attention to the courageous life which it has evoked and fostered. It is, however, perhaps significant that the adherents of war are more and more justifying it by its past record and reminding us of its ancient origin. They tell us that it is interwoven with every fibre of human growth and is at the root of all that is noble and courageous in human life, that struggle is the basis of all progress, that it is now extended from individuals and tribes to nations and races.

We may admire much that is admirable in this past life of courageous warfare while at the same time we accord it no right to dominate the present, which has traveled out of its reach into a land of new desires. We may admit that the experiences of war have equipped the men of the present with pluck and energy, but to insist upon the selfsame expression for that pluck and energy would be as stupid a mistake as if we would relegate the full-grown citizen, responding to many claims and demands upon his powers, to the school-yard fights of his boyhood, or to the college contests of his cruder youth. The little lad who stoutly defends himself on the school-ground may be worthy of much admiration, but if we find him, a dozen years later, the bullying leader of a street-gang who bases his prestige on the fact that "no one can whip him," our admiration cools amazingly, and we say that the carrying over of those puerile instincts into manhood shows arrested development which is mainly responsible for filling our prisons.

This confusion between the contemporaneous stage of development and the historic role of certain qualities, is intensified by our custom of referring to social evolution as if it were a force and not a process. We assume that social ends may be obtained without the application of social energies, although we know in our hearts that the best results of civilization have come about only through human will and effort. To point to the achievement of the past as a guarantee for continuing what has since become shocking to us is stupid business; it is to forget that progress itself depends upon adaptation, upon a nice balance between continuity and change. Let us by all means acknowledge and preserve that which has been good in warfare and in the spirit of warfare; let us gather it together and incorporate it in our national fibre. Let us, however, not be guilty for a moment of shutting our eyes to that which for many centuries must have been disquieting to the moral sense, but which is gradually becoming impossible, not only because of our increasing sensibilities, but because great constructive plans and humanized interests have captured our hopes and we are finding that war is an implement too clumsy and barbaric to subserve our purpose. We have come to realize that the great task of pushing forward social justice could be enormously accelerated if primitive methods as well as primitive weapons were once for all abolished.

The past may have been involved in war and suffering in order to bring forth a new and beneficent courage, an invincible ardor for conserving and healing human life, for understanding and elaborating it. To obtain this courage is to distinguish between a social order founded upon law enforced by authority and that other social order which includes liberty of individual action and complexity of group development. The latter social order would not suppress the least germ of promise, of growth and variety, but would nurture all into a full and varied life. It is not an easy undertaking to obtain it and it cannot be carried forward without conscious and well-defined effort. The task that is really before us is first to see to it, that the old virtues bequeathed by war are not retained after they have become a social deterrent and that social progress is not checked by a certain contempt for human nature which is but the inherited result of conquest. Second, we must act upon the assumption that spontaneous and fraternal action as virile and widespread as war itself is the only method by which substitutes for the war virtues may be discovered.

It was contended in the first chapter of this book that social morality is developed through sentiment and action. In this particular age we can live the truth which has been apprehended by our contemporaries, that truth which is especially our own, only by establishing nobler and wiser social relations and by discovering social bonds better fitted to our requirements. Warfare in the past has done much to bring men together. A sense of common danger and the stirring appeal to action for a common purpose, easily open the channels of sympathy through which we partake of the life about us. But there are certainly other methods of opening those channels. A social life to be healthy must be consciously and fully adjusted to the march of social needs, and as we may easily make a mistake by forgetting that enlarged opportunities are ever demanding an enlarged morality, so we will fail in the task of substitution if we do not demand social sympathy in a larger measure and of a quality better adapted to the contemporaneous situation. Perhaps the one point at which this undertaking is most needed is in regard to our conception of patriotism, which, although as genuine as ever before, is too much dressed in the trappings of the past and continually carries us back to its beginnings in military prowess and defence. To have been able to trace the origin and development of patriotism and then to rest content with that, and to fail to insist that it shall respond to the stimulus of a larger and more varied environment with which we are now confronted, is a confession of weakness; it exhibits lack of moral enterprise and of national vigor.

We have all seen the breakdown of village standards of morality when the conditions of a great city are encountered. To do "the good lying next at hand" may be a sufficient formula when the village idler and his needy children live but a few doors down the street, but the same dictum may be totally misleading when the villager becomes a city resident and finds his next-door neighbors prosperous and comfortable, while the poor and overburdened live many blocks away where he would never see them at all, unless he were stirred by a spirit of social enterprise to go forth and find them in the midst of their meagre living and their larger needs. The spirit of village gossip, penetrating and keen as it is, may be depended upon to bring to the notice of the kindhearted villager all cases of suffering—that someone is needed "to sit up all night" with a sick neighbor, or that the village loafer has been drunk again and beaten his wife; but in a city divided so curiously into the regions of the well-to-do and the congested quarters of the immigrant, the conscientious person can no longer rely upon gossip. There is no intercourse, not even a scattered one, between the two, save what the daily paper brings, with its invincible propensity to report the gossip of poverty and crime, perhaps a healthier tendency than we imagine. The man who has moved from the village to the cosmopolitan city and who would continue even his former share of beneficent activity must bestir himself to keep informed as to social needs and to make new channels through which his sympathy may flow. Without some such conscious effort, his sympathy will finally become stratified along the line of his social intercourse and he will be unable really to care for any people but his "own kind." American conceptions of patriotism have moved, so to speak, from the New England village into huge cosmopolitan cities. They find themselves bewildered by the change and have not only failed to make the adjustment, but the very effort in that direction is looked upon with deep suspicion by their old village neighbors. Unless our conception of patriotism is progressive, it cannot hope to embody the real affection and the real interest of the nation. We know full well that the patriotism of common descent is the mere patriotism of the clan—the early patriotism of the tribe—and that, while the possession of a like territory is an advance upon that first conception, both of them are unworthy to be the patriotism of a great cosmopolitan nation. We shall not have made any genuine advance until we have grown impatient of a patriotism founded upon military prowess and defence, because this really gets in the way and prevents the growth of that beneficent and progressive patriotism which we need for the understanding and healing of our current national difficulties.

To seek our patriotism in some age other than our own is to accept a code that is totally inadequate to help us through the problems which current life develops. We continue to found our patriotism upon war and to contrast conquest with nurture, militarism with industrialism, calling the latter passive and inert and the former active and aggressive, without really facing the situation as it exists. We tremble before our own convictions, and are afraid to find newer manifestations of courage and daring lest we thereby lose the virtues bequeathed to us by war. It is a pitiful acknowledgment that we have lost them already and that we shall have to give up the ways of war, if for no other reason than to preserve the finer spirit of courage and detachment which it has engendered and developed.

We come at last to the practical question as to how these substitutes for the war virtues may be found. How may we, the children of an industrial and commercial age, find the courage and sacrifice which belong to our industrialism. We may begin with August Comte's assertion that man seeks to improve his position in two different ways, by the destruction of obstacles and by the construction of means, or, designated by their most obvious social results, if his contention is correct, by military action and by industrial action, and that the two must long continue side by side. Then we find ourselves asking what may be done to make more picturesque those lives which are spent in a monotonous and wearing toil, compared to which the camp is exciting and the barracks comfortable. How shall it be made to seem as magnificent patiently to correct the wrongs of industrialism as to do battle for the rights of the nation? This transition ought not to be so difficult in America, for to begin with, our national life in America has been largely founded upon our success in invention and engineering, in manufacturing and commerce. Our prosperity has rested upon constructive labor and material progress, both of them in striking contrast to warfare. There is an element of almost grim humor in the nation's reverting at last to the outworn methods of battle-ships and defended harbors. We may admit that idle men need war to keep alive their courage and endurance, but we have few idle men in a nation engaged in industrialism. We constantly see subordination of sensation to sentiment in hundreds of careers which are not military; the thousands of miners in Pennsylvania doubtless endure every year more bodily pain and peril than the same number of men in European barracks.

Industrial life affords ample opportunity for endurance, discipline, and a sense of detachment, if the struggle is really put upon the highest level of industrial efficiency. But because our industrial life is not on this level, we constantly tend to drop the newer and less developed ideals for the older ones of warfare, we ignore the fact that war so readily throws back the ideals which the young are nourishing into the mold of those which the old should be outgrowing. It lures young men not to develop, but to exploit; it turns them from the courage and toil of industry to the bravery and endurance of war, and leads them to forget that civilization is the substitution of law for war. It incites their ambitions, not to irrigate, to make fertile and sanitary, the barren plain of the savage, but to fill it with military posts and tax-gatherers, to cease from pushing forward industrial action into new fields and to fall back upon military action.

We may illustrate this by the most beneficent acts of war, when the military spirit claiming to carry forward civilization invades a country for the purpose of bringing it into the zone of the civilized world. Militarism enforces law and order and insists upon obedience and discipline, assuming that it will ultimately establish righteousness and foster progress. In order to carry out this good intention, it first of all clears the decks of impedimenta, although in the process it may extinguish the most precious beginnings of self-government and the nucleus of self-help, which the wise of the native community have long been anxiously hoarding.

It is the military idea, resting content as it does with the passive results of order and discipline, which confesses a totally inadequate conception of the value and power of human life. The charge of obtaining negative results could with great candor he brought against militarism, while the strenuous task, the vigorous and difficult undertaking, involving the use of the most highly developed human powers, can be claimed for industrialism.

It is really human constructive labor which must give the newly invaded country a sense of its place in the life of the civilized world, some idea of the effective occupations which it may perform. In order to accomplish this its energy must be freed and its resources developed. Militarism undertakes to set in order, to suppress and to govern, if necessary to destroy, while industrialism undertakes to liberate latent forces, to reconcile them to new conditions, to demonstrate that their aroused activities can no longer follow caprice, but must fit into a larger order of life. To call this latter undertaking, demanding ever new powers of insight, patience, and fortitude, less difficult, less manly, less strenuous, than the first, is on the face of it absurd. It is the soldier who is inadequate to the difficult task, who strews his ways with blunders and lost opportunities, who cannot justify his vocation by the results, and who is obliged to plead guilty to a lack of rational method.

Of British government in the Empire, an Englishman has recently written, "We are obliged in practise to make a choice between good order and justice administered autocratically in accordance with British standards on the one hand, and delicate, costly, doubtful, and disorderly experiments in self-government on British lines upon the other, and we have practically everywhere decided upon the former alternative. It is, of course less difficult."[1] Had our American ideals of patriotism and morality in international relations kept pace with our experience, had we followed up our wide commercial relations with an adequate ethical code, we can imagine a body of young Americans, "the flower

1. *Imperialism,* by John A. Hobson, page 128.

of our youth," as we like to say, proudly declining commercial advantages founded upon forced military occupation and informing their well-meaning government that they declined to accept openings on any such terms as these, that their ideals of patriotism and of genuine government demanded the play of their moral prowess and their constructive intelligence. Certainly in America we have a chance to employ something more active and virile, more inventive, more in line with our temperament and tradition, than the mere desire to increase commercial relations by armed occupation as other governments have done. A different conduct is required from a democracy than from the mere order-keeping, bridge-building, tax-gathering Roman, or from the conscientious Briton carrying the blessings of an established government and enlarged commerce to all quarters of the globe.

It has been the time-honored custom to attribute unjust wars to the selfish ambition of rulers who remorselessly sacrifice their subjects to satisfy their greed. But, as Lecky has recently pointed out, it remains to be seen whether or not democratic rule will diminish war. Immoderate and uncontrolled desires are at the root of most national as well as of most individual crimes, and a large number of persons may be moved by unworthy ambitions quite as easily as a few. If the electorate of a democracy accustom themselves to take the commercial view of life, to consider the extension of trade as the test of a national prosperity, it becomes comparatively easy for mere extension of commercial opportunity to assume a moral aspect and to receive the moral sanction. Unrestricted commercialism is an excellent preparation for governmental aggression. The nation which is accustomed to condone the questionable business methods of a rich man because of his success, will find no difficulty in obscuring the moral issues involved in any undertaking that is successful. It becomes easy to deny the moral basis of self-government and to substitute militarism. The soldier formerly looked down upon the merchant whom he now obeys, as he still looks down upon the laborer as a man who is engaged in a business inferior to his own, as someone who is dull and passive and ineffective. When our public education succeeds in freeing the creative energy and developing the skill which the advance of industry demands, this attitude must disappear, and a spectacle such as that recently seen in London among the idle men returned from service in South Africa, who refused to work through a contemptuous attitude towards the "slow life" of the laborer, will become impossible. We have as yet failed to uncover the relative difficulty and requisite training for the two methods of life.

It is difficult to illustrate on a national scale the substitution of the ideals of labor for those of warfare.

At the risk of being absurd, and with the certainty of pushing an illustration beyond its legitimate limits, I am venturing to typify this substitution by the one man whom the civilized world has most closely associated with military ideals, the present Emperor of Germany. We may certainly believe that the German Emperor is a conscientious man, who means to do his duty to all his subjects; that he regards himself, not only as general and chief of the army, but also as the fostering father of the humble people. Let us imagine the quite impossible thing that for ten years he does not review any troops, does not attend any parades, does not wear a uniform, nor hear the clang of the sword as he walks, but that during these ten years he lives with the peasants "who drive the painful plow," that he constantly converses with them, and subjects himself to their alternating hopes and fears as to the result of the harvest, at best so inadequate for supplying their wants and for paying their taxes. Let us imagine that the German Emperor during these halcyon years, in addition to the companionship of the humble, reads only the folk-lore, the minor poetry and the plaintive songs in which German literature is so rich, until he comes to see each man of the field as he daily goes forth to his toil "with a soldier tied to his back," exhausted by the double strain of his burden and his work.

Let us imagine this Emperor going through some such profound moral change as befell Count Tolstoy when he quitted his military service in the Caucasus and lived with the peasants on his estate, with this difference that, instead of feeling directly responsible for a village of humble folk, he should come to feel responsible for all the toilers of the "Fatherland" and for the international results of the German army. Let us imagine that in his self-surrender to the humblest of his people, there would gradually grow up in his subconsciousness, forces more ideal than any which had possessed him before; that his interests and thoughts would gradually shift from war and the manoeuvres and extensions of the army, to the unceasing toil, the permanent patience, which lie at the bottom of all national existence; that the life of the common people, which is so infinite in its moral suggestiveness, would open up to him new moral regions, would stir new energies within him, until there would take place one of those strange alterations in personality of which hundreds of examples are recorded. Under a glow of generous indignation, magnanimity, loyalty to his people, a passion of self-surrender to his new ideals, we can imagine that the imperial temperament would waste no time in pinings and regret, but that, his energies being enlisted in an overmastering desire to free the people from the burden of the army, he would drive vigorously in the direction of his new ideals. It is impossible to imagine him "passive" under this conversion to the newer ideals of peace. He would no more be passive than St. Paul was after his conversion. He would regard the four million men in Europe shut up in barracks, fed in idleness by toiling peasants, as an actual wrong and oppression. They would all have to be freed and returned to normal life and occupation—not through the comparatively easy method of storming garrisons, in which he has had training, but through conviction on the part of rulers and people of the wrong and folly of barrack idleness and military glitter. The freeing of the Christians from the oppressions of the Turks, of the Spaniards from the Moslems, could offer no more strenuous task—always, however, with the added difficulty and complication that the change in the people must be a moral change analogous to the one which had already taken place within himself; that he must be debarred from the use of weapons, to which his earlier life had made him familiar; that his high task, while enormous in its proportion, was still most delicate in its character, and must be undertaken without the guarantee of precedent, and without any surety of success. "Smitten with the great vision of social righteousness," as so many of his contemporaries have been, he could not permit himself to be blinded or to take refuge in glittering generalities, but, even as St. Paul arose from his vision and went on his way in a new determination never again changed, so he would have to go forth to a mission, imperial indeed in its magnitude, but "over-imperial" in the sweep of its consequences and in the difficulty of its accomplishment.

Certainly counting all the hours of the Emperor's life spent in camp and court dominated by military pomp and ambition, he has given more than ten years to military environment and much less than ten years to the bulk of his people, and it would not be impossible to imagine such a conversion due to the reaction of environment and interest. Such a change having taken place, should we hold him royal in temper or worthy of the traditions of knight-errantry, if he were held back by commercial considerations, if he hesitated because the Krupp Company could sell no more guns and would be thrown out of business? We should say to this Emperor whom our imaginations have evoked, Were your enthusiasms genuine enough, were your insights absolutely true, you would see of how little consequence these things really are, and how easily adjusted. Let the Krupp factories, with their tremendous resources in machinery and men, proceed to manufacture dredging machines for the reclaiming of the waste land in Posen; let them make new inventions to relieve the drudgery of the peasant, agricultural implements adequate to Germany's agricultural resources and possibilities. They will find need for all the power of invention which they can command, all the manufacturing and commercial ability which they now employ. It is part of your new vocation to adjust the industries now tributary to the standing armies and organization of warfare, to useful and beneficent occupations; to transform and readjust all their dependent industries, from the manufacturing of cannon and war-ships to that of gold braid and epaulets. It is your mission to revive and increase agriculture, industry, and commerce, by diverting all the energy which is now directed to the feeding, clothing, and arming of the idle, into the legitimate and normal channels of life.

It is certainly not more difficult to imagine such a change occurring to an entire people than in the mind and purpose of one man—in fact, such changes are going on all about us.

The advance of constructive labor and the subsidence and disappearance of destructive warfare is a genuine line of progression. One sees much of protection and something of construction in the office of war, as the Roman bridges survived throughout Europe long after the legions which built them and crossed them for new conquests had passed out of mind. Also, in the rising tide of labor there is a large admixture of warfare, of the purely militant spirit which is sometimes so dominant that it throws the entire movement into confusion and leads the laborer to renounce his birthright; but nevertheless the desire for battle is becoming constantly more restricted in area. It still sways in regions where men of untamed blood are dwelling and among men who, because they regard themselves as a superior race, imagine that they are free from the ordinary moral restraints; but its territory constantly grows smaller and its manifestations more guarded. Doubtless war will exist for many generations among semi-savage tribes, and it will also break out in those nations which may be roused and dominated by the unrestricted commercial spirit; but the ordinary life of man will go on without it, as it becomes transmitted into a desire for normal human relationship.

It is difficult to predict at what moment the conviction that war is foolish or wasteful or unjustifiable may descend upon the earth, and it is also impossible to estimate among how many groups of people this conviction has already become established.

The Doukhobors are a religious sect in Russia whose creed emphasizes the teaching of non-resistance. A story is told of one of their young men who, because of his refusal to enter the Russian army, was brought for trial before a judge, who reasoned with him concerning the folly of his course and in return received a homily upon the teachings of Jesus. "Quite right you are," answered the judge, "from the point of abstract virtue, but the time has not yet come to put into practise the literal sayings of Christ." "The time may not have come for you, your Honor," was the reply, "but the time has come for us." Who can tell at what hour vast numbers of Russian peasants upon those Russian steppes will decide that the time has come for them to renounce warfare, even as their prototype, the mujik, Count Tolstoy, has already decided that it has come for him? Conscious as the peasants are of religious motive, they will meet a cheerful martyrdom for their convictions, as so many of the Doukhobors have done. It may, however, be easy to overestimate this changed temper because of the simple yet dramatic formulation given by Tolstoy to the non-resisting spirit. How far Tolstoy is really the mouthpiece of a great moral change going on in the life of the Russian peasant and how far he speaks merely for himself, it is, of course, impossible to state. If only a few peasants are experiencing this change, his genius has certainly done much to make their position definite. The man who assumes that a new degree of virtue is possible, thereby makes it real and tangible to those who long to possess it but lack courage. Tolstoy at least is ready to predict that in the great affairs of national disarmament, it may easily be true that the Russian peasants will take the first steps.

Their armed rebellion may easily be overcome by armed troops, but what can be done with their permanent patience, their insatiable hunger for holiness? All idealism has its prudential aspects, and, as has been pointed out by Mr. Perris,[2] no other form of revolution is so fitted to an agricultural people as this continued outburst of passive resistance among whole communities, not in theory, but in practise. This peasant movement goes on in spite of persecution, perfectly spontaneous, self-reliant, colossal in the silent confidence and power of endurance. In this day of Maxim guns and high explosives, the old method of revolt would be impossible to an agricultural people, but the non-resistant strike against military service lies directly in line with the temperament and capacity of the Russian people. That "the government cannot put the whole population in prison, and, if it could, it would still be without material for an army, and without money for its support," is an almost irrefutable argument. We see here, at least, the beginnings of a sentiment that shall, if sufficiently developed, make war impossible to an entire people, a conviction of sin manifesting itself throughout a nation.

Whatever may have been true of the revolutionist of the past when his spike was on a certain level of equality with the bayonet of the regular soldier, and his enthusiasm and daring could, in large measure, overcome the difference, it is certainly true now that such simple arms as a revolutionist could command, would be utterly futile against the equipment of the regular soldier. To continue the use of armed force means, under these circumstances, that we must refer the possibilities of all social and industrial advance to the consent of the owners of the Maxim guns. We must deny to the humble the possibility of the initiation of progressive movements employing revolution or, at least, we must defer all advance until the humble many can persuade the powerful few of the righteousness of their cause, and we must throw out the working class from participation in the beginnings of social revolutions. Tolstoy would make non-resistance aggressive. He would carry over into the reservoirs of moral influence all the strength which

2. *The Grand Mujik,* G. H. Perris.

is now spent in coercion and resistance. It is an experiment which in its fullness has never been tried in human history, and it is worthy of a genius. As moral influence has ever a larger place in individual relationship and as physical force becomes daily more restricted in area, so Tolstoy would "speed up" the process in collective relationships and reset the whole of international life upon the basis of good will and intelligent understanding. It does not matter that he has entered these new moral fields through the narrow gateway of personal experience; that he sets forth his convictions with the limitations of the Russian governmental environment; that he is regarded at this moment by the Russian revolutionists as a quietist and reactionary. He has nevertheless reached down into the moral life of the humble people and formulated for them as for us the secret of their long patience and unremitting labor. Therefore, in the teachings of Tolstoy, as in the life of the peasants, coextensive with the doctrine of non-resistance, stress is laid upon productive labor. The peasant Bandereff, from whom Tolstoy claims to have learned much, has not only proclaimed himself as against war, but has written a marvelous book entitled "Bread Labor," expressing once more the striking antithesis, the eternal contrast between war and labor, and between those who abhor the one and ever advocate the other.

War on the one hand—plain destruction, Von Moltke called it— represents the life of the garrison and the tax-gatherer, the Roman emperor and his degenerate people, living upon the fruits of their conquest. Labor, on the other hand, represents productive effort, holding carefully what has been garnered by the output of brain and muscle, guarding the harvest jealously because it is the precious bread men live by.

It is quite possible that we have committed the time-honored folly of looking for a sudden change in men's attitude toward war, even as the poor alchemists wasted their lives in searching for a magic fluid and did nothing to discover the great laws governing chemical changes and reactions, the knowledge of which would have developed untold wealth beyond their crude dreams of transmuted gold.

The final moral reaction may at last come, accompanied by deep remorse, too tardy to reclaim all the human life which has been spent and the treasure which has been wasted, or it may come with a great

sense of joy that all voluntary destruction of human life, all the delib-
erate wasting of the fruits of labor, have become a thing of the past,
and that whatever the future contains for us, it will at least be free from
war. We may at last comprehend the truth of that which Ruskin has
stated so many times, that we worship the soldier, not because he goes
forth to slay, but to be slain.

That this world peace movement should be arising from the humblest without the sanction and in some cases with the explicit indifference, of the church founded by the Prince of Peace, is simply another
example of the strange paths of moral evolution.

To some of us it seems clear that marked manifestations of this
movement are found in the immigrant quarters of American cities.
The previous survey of the immigrant situation would indicate that
all the peoples of the world have become part of the American tribunal, and that their sense of pity, their clamor for personal kindness,
their insistence upon the right to join in our progress, can no longer
be disregarded. The burdens and sorrows of men have unexpectedly
become intelligent and urgent to this nation, and it is only by accepting them with some magnanimity that we can develop the larger sense
of justice which is becoming world-wide and is lying in ambush, as it
were, to manifest itself in governmental relations. Men of all nations
are determining upon the abolition of degrading poverty, disease, and
intellectual weakness, with their resulting industrial inefficiency, and
are making a determined effort to conserve even the feeblest citizen to
the State. To join in this determined effort is to break through national
bonds and to unlock the latent fellowship between man and man. In
a political campaign men will go through every possible hardship in
response to certain political loyalties; in a moment of national danger
men will sacrifice every personal advantage. It is but necessary to make
this fellowship wider, to extend its scope without lowering its intensity.
Those emotions which stir the spirit to deeds of self-surrender and to
high enthusiasm, are among the world's most precious assets. That this
emotion has so often become associated with war, by no means proves
that it cannot be used for other ends. There is something active and
tangible in this new internationalism, although it is difficult to make it
clear, and in our striving for a new word with which to express this new
and important sentiment, we are driven to the rather absurd phrase of

"cosmic patriotism." Whatever it may be called, it may yet be strong enough to move masses of men out of their narrow national considerations and cautions into new reaches of human effort and affection. Religion has long ago taught that only as the individual can establish a sense of union with a power for righteousness not himself, can he experience peace; and it may be possible that the nations will be called to a similar experience.

The International Peace Conference held in Boston in 1904 was opened by a huge meeting in which men of influence and modern thought from four continents, gave reasons for their belief in the passing of war. But none was so modern, so fundamental and so trenchant, as the address which was read from the prophet Isaiah. He founded the cause of peace upon the cause of righteousness, not only as expressed in political relations, but also in industrial relations. He contended that peace could be secured only as men abstained from the gains of oppression and responded to the cause of the poor; that swords would finally be beaten into plowshares and pruning-hooks, not because men resolved to be peaceful, but because all the metal of the earth would be turned to its proper use when the poor and their children should be abundantly fed. It was as if the ancient prophet foresaw that under an enlightened industrialism peace would no longer be an absence of war, but the unfolding of worldwide processes making for the nurture of human life. He predicted the moment which has come to us now that peace is no longer an abstract dogma but has become a rising tide of moral enthusiasm slowly engulfing all pride of conquest and making war impossible.

Index

26; social problems not settled by, 114; strikes as, 61, 72–75; substitutes for virtues of, 120–21; and taxation, 129; tribal, 127; unjust, attributed to ambitious ruler, 123–24; workers' opposition to, xxii. *See also* capitalism; industrialism; labor; moral substitutes for war; pacifism

Warne, F. J., 54

Webb, Beatrice, 106

Weber, A. T., 12

Weinberg, Arthur and Lila, lv, lxxii n. 99

Wells-Barnett, Ida B., xlv, xlvi–xlvii, lxviii n. 52, lxix n. 59–60

Whipps, Judy D., lxxii n. 95

Whitman, Walt, 27

Wilcox, Delos F., 32, 65

Wilson, Woodrow, lx

Wollstonecraft, Mary, lxv n. 18

woman suffrage: denial of, xl, lxviii n. 49; education and, lxi, 104; and infant mortality, 103; militarism and denial of franchise for women, 101–03; questions about, 103–04; rationale for, 101–02, 106, 109, 113

women: Addams vs. James on, xxxii; African American, and Addams, xlv–xlvii, lxviii–lxix n. 52, n. 54, n. 58, n. 60; changed conditions of food preparation by, 104–05; as employers, 76, 109–10, 111; German, alleged sexual assault on, lxix n. 58; inclusion in decision-making, lxi–lxii, 101, 102; municipal government and, xxiii, 100–15; *Notable American*, lii, lxxi n. 85; need for industrial era education of, xli, 104, 109, 111–12, 113–14; outmoded conventions harmful to, 103; and overcoming military virtues, xxx; patriotism of, 42; at Peace Congress 1904, xxvii; in peace movement, l, lv–lvi, lxx n. 75, lxxiii n. 115; public responsibilities and rights of, xiv, lvii, lxv n. 16, 18, 102–04, 106, 109, 113–15; as social

theorists, lii, liii–lv, lxxi n. 90–91; status and roles of, xl–xli, 101–05. *See also* International Women's Working Conference; woman suffrage; women workers

Women's International League for Peace and Freedom, lxv n. 9, lxix n. 58

women workers: action needed by well-informed, xl, 106; denied control over changed conditions of life and work in factory system, xl–xli, 104–05; as domestic workers, 109–10; effects of machinery on, 105; as electors, 114–15; in garment industry, 106–09; intelligence of, xl–xli; labor dispute of, 66–67; increasing numbers of, 105; as percentage of work force, compared to men, 105; protective legislation for, 106, 109; spinning processes, 112, 113

working classes, xxxi: disinterest in electoral politics, xxxvi, 48; exploitation of, xx; fate of, 81; ignored by government, 47–49; immigrants as coming together with, 53–62, 64–65; immigration problem as perceived by, 52–53; on industrialism, xxv–xxvi; as opponents of militarism and imperialism, xxi–xxii, 63; protections for, 50–51; standard of living for, 64–65. *See also* industrialism; labor; masses

workingmen: employers on, 76–78; International Association of Workingmen (London), xxii, xxvii, lxvii n. 29, 63; first to formulate new internationalism, xxvii; peace movement to be in hands of, xxvii

Workman's Peace Association, lxvii n. 33

World Social Forum (2003), lxii

Wright, Quincy, xvii, lxv n. 17

Zinn, Howard, lv

Zwick, Jim, lxiv–lxv n. 9

JANE ADDAMS (1860–1935) was a social activist, a leading Progressive reformer, public speaker, author of many books of social criticism, and an original theorist who contributed to the development of American sociology and pragmatist philosophy. Her feminism, pacifism, and pragmatist experimentalism found concrete expression in the institutions she founded or to which she gave early support, including the Hull-House settlement in Chicago, the National Association for the Advancement of Colored People, the National American Woman Suffrage Association, the American Civil Liberties Union, and the Women's International League for Peace and Freedom. She was awarded the Nobel Peace Prize in 1931.

BERENICE A. CARROLL is a professor of political science and women's studies at Purdue University and professor emerita at the University of Illinois at Urbana-Champaign. She is past president of the National Women's Studies Association. Her books and articles include *Design for Total War: Arms and Economics in the Third Reich, Liberating Women's History: Theoretical and Critical Essays, Women's Political and Social Thought* (co-edited with Hilda L. Smith), "The Politics of 'Originality': Women and the Class System of Intellect," and "Christine de Pizan and the Origins of Peace Theory."

CLINTON F. FINK is a visiting scholar in sociology/anthropology at Purdue University. He is past co-chair and executive director of the Consortium on Peace Research, Education, and Development, and former editor of the *Journal of Conflict Resolution* and the *COPRED Peace Chronicle*. His publications include *Peace and War: A Guide to Bibliographies* (with Berenice A. Carroll and Jane E. Mohraz), *Peace Research in Transition* (co-editor with Elise Boulding), "Some Conceptual Difficulties in the Theory of Social Conflict," and "Confronting Columbusism: Peace Education and the 500 Year Crisis."

The University of Illinois Press
is a founding member of the
Association of American University Presses.

University of Illinois Press
1325 South Oak Street
Champaign, IL 61820-6903
www.press.uillinois.edu